D1586590

Farewell my child

Stories told and memories
cherished, shared experiences of
child bereavement

Copyright © 2008 Child Bereavement Charity

Edited by Ann Chalmers

Published by
Child Bereavement Charity

Aston ' Child Bereavement Charity ' Wycombe,
Buckir The Saunderton Estate
Telept Wycombe Road, Saunderton
Buckinghamshire HP14 4BF
Fax 01 Tel: 01494 568900
Websi www.childbereavement.org.uk nt.org.uk

First published 2008
ISBN number 978-0-9521661-7-7

Body text set in Sari Regular 11/14pt

Produced by Ethedo Press

With grateful thanks to
Barclays Financial Planning
for their support of this project

This paper is made from
pulp originating from
certified sustainable forests

This book is dedicated to

Liam Logue, a much loved and missed brother and son,
whose loss inspired fundraising for this book
and in doing so creates a lasting memorial

and

Ellen Ruth Poll, a beautiful daughter and sister,
whose legacy has helped raise so much for others in need of support,
and who still lives very much in the hearts and minds
of her family every day

With grateful thanks to all the families who have contributed
in memory of their precious children

Contents

Foreword 6
Ann Chalmers
Chief Executive, Child Bereavement Charity

A personal journey 7
Jenni Thomas OBE
Founder and President, Child Bereavement Charity

Introduction 10
Nicholas Timothy Charles Knatchbull
Countess Mountbatten of Burma CBE CD JP DL

Coping with loss 13
Maksim Tadeusz Szpojnarowicz
Sonya Szpojnarowicz
President, Child Bereavement Support (Singapore)

Farewell my child

Sebastian Gabriel Beckley 22

Billie Eve Buckley 28

Tom Clabburn 33

Lucy S.O. Empson 37

Thomas Henry Fone 41

Frederick George Arthur Greenwood 47

Misha Hannah and Natalie India Griffith 49

Hazel Guinn 56

Sabah Tanya Hussain 61

Lewie Steven Charlie Jones 67

Angus Lawson 76

Zoe Le	81
Liam Francis Logue	84
Rose Markwort	92
Benedict "Benny" Martin Leo May	99
Rosie Mayling	108
Annabelle Alice McCabe	113
Mary Caitlin Neill	119
James Aidan Pearson	123
Ned Stanley Rufus Pennant	132
Ellen Ruth Poll	137
Thomas Joseph Rodin	145
Adelina Scott Lin	148
Harry Charles Chappe Sidebottom	155
Abigail Slatter	162
Callum David Anders Smith	169
Guy Sobel	175
Betsy Louise and William John Woodbridge	179
Organisations that can help	185
Useful resources	189

Foreword

The relationship between parent and child is unique. The death of a baby or child at whatever age leaves parents searching for meaning and wondering how they will ever live life again in the face of such pain and anguish, and families have often wanted to know how others have survived such a tragedy. The Child Bereavement Charity bases everything it does on learning from families, and it therefore seemed important to find a way of giving families the opportunity to share with and help others by telling us about their experiences.

The Child Bereavement Charity has, for several years, had a link with families in Singapore and in 2004 helped establish Child Bereavement Support (Singapore), founded by five bereaved mothers. The original *Farewell, My Child* was produced by this group's President, Sonya Szpojnarowicz, and continues to be an invaluable support to families. We thank Sonya for her encouragement as we developed this UK version of the book.

We have been fortunate in being helped not only by the many families who have contributed to this book, but particularly by the families of Liam Logue and Ellen Poll who raised funds in their memory to make this resource possible. The extraordinary courage of all who have so generously given of themselves in sharing their precious children is immense. Our thanks seem so inadequate, but are heartfelt.

I am sure those who read this book will find something to identify with and hope that in some small way they will find within its pages some comfort and hope for the future.

Ann Chalmers
Chief Executive
Child Bereavement Charity

A personal journey

People have often asked me over the 40 years I have worked in the NHS, why I became involved in working with bereaved families. They imagine perhaps I have experienced the loss of a child myself. However it was only when I trained as a counsellor in 1980 that I began to understand my own childhood experience of loss and bereavement.

I became aware that the death of my father during the war, when I was two, had affected me in many ways. Obviously I do not remember him, but the effect of growing up in a family where my Mother was grieving deeply, not only for him but also for her only brother who had been killed a few months earlier, pervaded our lives. I understand now that our family was in mourning during my childhood. My younger sister was born a few days before my father was killed. Two very important family members had died and the space they left was enormous. I don't remember ever talking about feelings as a child, but as the eldest I can only recall an overwhelming sadness that I didn't understand. I do remember very much wanting to make it better for my Mother. I think that was where the taking care of people started, where the carer in me began.

The other revelation from my counselling training was that, having spent many years working in hospitals looking after dying babies and children, I had never thought of myself as a bereaved child. I had had no training in understanding loss and grief as a healthcare professional. We were just expected to know how to deal with death, with distress. After all we were there to look after people; we should just know what to do. No one I worked with, not even the doctors, had any training in bereavement and most professionals felt hugely inadequate. All we had was our caring and humanity. In those days, and still often today, it was not considered professional to show emotion. We had to appear untouched by the death of a child or we were not being professional.

In truth, I noticed that the families appreciated staff that were able to show feelings and say how sorry they were that a precious child had died. The staff that distanced themselves and appeared unfeeling made it harder for families. Yet these professionals had often themselves experienced difficulties in their

7

personal life and were often unaware of the effect this was having on them and the way they worked. Through my training I learned the value of feeling an emotional response, and to appropriately show how I felt without losing control. Families had told me how helpful it was when doctors and nurses showed their humanity and expressed some emotion. I wanted to do counselling training to help me understand people, and in many ways it did – but most of all it taught me about myself and why I was drawn to bereavement work. This new awareness left me questioning the whole culture within the healthcare system.

For far too long, the emphasis has been on the technical success of medical treatment – yet we cannot separate medical care and emotional care. They are both fundamental to our well-being. My quest to change the system began its long journey – death and dying had to be acknowledged as important areas for all healthcare professionals.

Following on from my counselling training, I had to negotiate with senior management how I could provide bereavement counselling for families. This was indeed pioneering work with many obstacles to be overcome. One of the biggest problems for healthcare professionals generally was that it was not seen as a strength to need support in our working lives. If we showed distress when a patient died, very often we became the casualty in managers' eyes. Yet it is a strength to ask for support, not a weakness. I believed it should be a fundamental part of every professional carer's experience to be supported and trained in coming alongside bereaved families, to look at ourselves and to be self-aware, to consider what may have led us to train as doctors or nurses, and to enable us to give the best possible care to grieving families.

I began by counselling parents whose infants had died on the neonatal or maternity units soon after birth. My manager had the vision to see this was something the parents valued and encouraged me to establish a bereavement service within the hospital.

That initial support and commitment from my manager has led to much more. In 1994, I founded The Child Bereavement Trust, (now Child Bereavement Charity) to take forward this much needed work of supporting families and professionals. The charity has been able to establish training and support for professionals at many levels, across the UK and internationally. Our work has spread throughout the NHS, the voluntary sector, police, schools, reaching out to all those whose work involves bereavement. In 2000 I was honoured

8

to receive the inaugural Nye Bevan Lifetime Achievement Award for my work within the NHS.

Despite all this experience, nothing could have prepared me for the call that came from my youngest son telling me that he and his wife were on their way to hospital – the hospital I am based in. His wife was in premature labour at just under 24 weeks, and they asked me to be with them. Walking into that hospital, where I had so many times before been part of the team supporting bereaved families, felt so different when it was my little grandchild who was being born just too early. All the things I'd learnt that were important to other families suddenly became hugely significant in this, our family crisis.

Annabelle was born alive a few hours later and lived for just a short while. It mattered so much that her other Granny and Grandpa were also there, able to marvel at how tiny, perfect and just like her big sister Estelle she was. As a mother, I felt overwhelming sadness for my son and truly lovely daughter-in-law; as a granny, I felt huge sadness for all Annabelle would not experience in life. I just wanted to pick her up and take her home, pretend everything was going to be all right. I would have done anything in my power to make things better, but the many hundreds of families I have seen over  the years have taught me that this just can't be – there is no making it better. But three years on, much of the pain has lessened and the birth of a little grandson Dominic at 26 weeks – who thankfully survived – has helped to keep us all occupied and moving forward, never forgetting Annabelle who will always be my 6th grandchild. I feel immensely privileged to have been included in her short life.

Now in this month of my retirement, as *Farewell My Child* is published, I am so pleased the experiences of bereaved families will continue to be at the forefront of everything the Child Bereavement Charity does. I look forward to supporting the charity in whatever way I can and enjoying more quality time with my children and grandchildren.

Jenni Thomas OBE
Founder and President, Child Bereavement Charity

Nicholas Timothy Charles Knatchbull

18 November 1964 – 27 August 1979

I am so very pleased the varied accounts in this book may be the means of helping someone along the seemingly endless black tunnel towards the light that truly does appear at the end, and which we eventually found ourselves.

The loss of our beloved 14-year old identical twin, Nicholas, was through the detonated explosion of an IRA bomb on our small boat in Ireland on 27th August 1979.

The target was my 79-year old father, Earl Mountbatten of Burma, but Nicky, my dear 83-year old mother-in-law and a 15-year old Irish boy, Paul Maxwell, died also. The other twin, Timothy, my husband and I were very severely wounded and nearly died too.

We had all been out fishing in Donegal Bay in our old 30ft fishing boat, Shadow V. Luckily it was a very fine and calm Bank Holiday Monday with several small craft around, and those people in them gallantly helped to pull us from the sea or we would have drowned. The bomb had been placed under the floorboards of the boat and was detonated from the shore by people clearly able to see who was in the boat, which disintegrated into splinters. My own memory is of a vision of a ball exploding upwards and then "coming to" in the sea and wondering if I would be able to reach the surface before I passed out. I have very vague memories now and again of floating among the wood and debris, being pulled into a small rubber dinghy before totally losing consciousness for days until I regained it in Sligo Hospital in Intensive Care.

I thought the engine of the boat had exploded and only realised how serious the situation was when I heard someone say (thinking I was unconscious, and referring to my mother-in-law) "the old lady is dead". I then thought perhaps my father was too, at his age, but was not able to open my eyes or speak.

In my conscious intervals I began to realise Timothy was in the same room and I was told my husband was nearby – but no one mentioned Nicky. I gradually

realised that must be because he was dead, and managed to scrawl on a piece of paper later, when I felt strong enough to survive the news, "I think Nicky dead" to my visiting sister, who alas had to confirm it.

As anyone whose child dies will know only too well, this news utterly devastated me and I grieved so much for Nicky that I later began to feel guilty that I was not able to grieve so overwhelmingly for my father, who I really adored.

I was also desperately worried how darling Tim was going to cope with losing an inseparable twin and companion in everything they did together. I also worried later that he was being too brave in coping with his loss, and indeed it took him several years - despite his apparent stoicism - to come properly to terms with it and of course he will always feel that loss. But I am thankful his attitude is to live his life as two people and not as half a person and to make the best of everything.

I cried every morning on waking for about six months and found it difficult to feel any happiness for a year, (not helped by still being in a wheelchair or on

11

crutches for months) and it was two years before I felt I was probably "as good as it gets". I was tremendously lucky in having a wonderfully loving and understanding husband who suffered similarly, and also a marvellously supportive family in the other five children. But I again felt guilty that my own grief had been so overwhelming, it made me selfish in not fully realising the great sorrow suffered by all the family.

Of course I have learnt from our own experience of grief to instinctively realise how other people in circumstances of loss must be feeling, and to appreciate the immense value of being able to talk to another bereaved person without having to explain the various problems along the path to recovery, because they will understand.

For us, being able to keep Nicky's memory alive and very much part of our family circle by being talked about and remembered, was all-important. When asked how many children I have I usually say "I had seven" or "I have six down here and one in heaven".

Birth and death are both the key elements of life and it seems wrong to be afraid to face a death, thereby helping to erase a much loved memory.

After our tragedy a very kind and understanding stranger sent me from China a translated poem she had found there amongst ancient archives.

He has gone into another room
I cannot find
But I know he was here
Because of all the happiness
He left behind

We thought it so beautiful and comforting we inscribed it on Nicky's tombstone.

Patricia Mountbatten of Burma
Honorary President
Child Bereavement Charity

12

Maksim Tadeusz Szpojnarowicz

5 May 2000 - 17 April 2002

Chris and Sonya are English expatriates who have lived in Singapore for twelve years. Max was their first child, a beautiful, happy, healthy little boy who brought them enormous joy. Their lives were turned upside down when Max suddenly died, peacefully, in his sleep just over two weeks before his 2nd birthday. There was no warning – he had only shown 'normal' cold symptoms for a few days.

Sonya interviewed families for the original 'Farewell, My Child' written in 2005 for Child Bereavement Support (Singapore). The following is adapted from that publication:

COPING WITH LOSS

The awful reality of losing a beloved child is something we face with extreme difficulty. But it IS possible to keep on living, slowly learning to accept it and eventually finding some kind of personal peace or closure. It is very important to remember to take one day at a time. From our various experiences we have gathered together some thoughts on things we found helpful to keep us going – or things we wish we'd known at the time:

He will always be your child

You will never stop loving your child, nor being his parent, just because he is no longer with you – this brings both pain and comfort. It means that you live with the pain of your child's loss forever, and that your heart will always yearn for him to come back. But it also means that you have a very special bond with your child that stays with you always. No one can ever take away your memories, your dreams and your love for your child.

No "right" or "wrong" way to grieve

Everyone will grieve in his or her own individual way – it is important to remember that there is no "right" or "wrong" way to grieve. There are "patterns" of grief, often referred to as "stages" (we will not go into these in detail as there are so many books that do this very well already), but many grieving parents will not go through these "stages" in the typical order described in many grief books.

> *"I know that I often felt that I was going through many 'stages' all at once, and that one day I seemed to be in one stage, and another day it seemed that I had gone back to what was supposed to be a much earlier stage. It was frightening to feel so lost and out of control. I could feel brave and strong one minute, looking to the outside world as if I was coping well – and then suddenly find myself in floods of tears for no clearly apparent reason. Likewise, there were times when I wanted so much to cry openly, when a kind friend was being supportive and I wanted to open up about how utterly awful I felt – but I couldn't take off my brave face."*
>
> ***Sonya***

It is also important to stress that you have to grieve as YOU feel you need to – no matter if others might expect something different or might consider you selfish for not following their expectations or customs.

> *"Often the bereaved are expected to follow with tradition and do certain 'stuff', but if that is not right for you, do what is, and don't feel the need to follow on as tradition dictates. Others CAN NOT understand, so don't worry about fitting their agenda. It is hard to defy common practice and family rituals but the family has likely not experienced this loss before. Do things in your time and do what you see fit."*
>
> ***Stefanie***

Allow yourself time

One thing that is very important is to be patient with yourself and give yourself time to grieve. It can be very damaging to feel that you "ought" to have got over it and to have "moved on". Experts agree that it takes many years for a bereaved parent to work through the grief process. So much will depend on the particular circumstances and so many things can complicate the process and serve to make it harder and longer. Added complications and sources of pain include babies that are stillborn, where the mother has had to give birth to death; children who have died particularly painful or horrific deaths; death of an only child or much longed for and difficult to conceive child; and parents who suffer guilt over their child's death - maybe they felt they failed to spot symptoms, failed to protect their child, should never have let them go out on their own...

Go with the flow

Grief is a frightening new universe. You might be used to feeling "in control", feeling confident in facing the world, proud and strong and invincible - and now suddenly you might feel totally lost, powerless and terrified. Try not to worry about feeling out of control - allow yourself to go with the flow. One mother hid away under the covers in her darkened room, taking a long time to emerge very slowly into the outside world. Sonya recalls how she took to wearing glasses instead of her usual contact lenses - so that she could take them off and "zone out" the world, sending everything into soft focus. She says, "I felt as if I wanted to hide away in a dark hole and not look anybody in the eyes ever again." All this is OK. Grief for a lost child is agony - there is nothing wrong with howling, crying hysterically, hiding away - do what you have to do to get through each moment.

The only way is through it

There are no short cuts to grieving - it is a natural, unavoidable process, and part of life. Taking medication may be a temporary fix but it will not solve the problem and one day you will have to face life without that help. We have to face up to the reality of our child's death, and to go through the pain of grieving their loss, if we are ever to find any kind of resolution and be able to move on with our lives with any kind of meaning. Facing up to the reality means things like seeing and touching your child's body, putting their possessions away, and talking openly about your child and about how you feel.

Pace yourself

While you have to go through it, you don't have to deal with it all at once. It is equally important to "pace" yourself over your loss. If you don't feel you are strong enough yet to pack away his things, or look at his video, you don't need to do it now. One mother took two years before she could watch a video of her child. And some parents prefer to leave their child's room intact instead

15

of putting away their things. Remember that you can revisit these issues when you feel stronger, even if it means taking years to mull over them. It's OK. But you will need to go through it at your own pace.

Be patient and kind, and nurture yourself
Whatever the circumstances, you must be patient and kind with yourself – and with your partner. The death of a child can put unbearable stress on the relationship of the parents, as you have both suffered an unbearable loss and so in many ways are both unable to help each other, whilst both needing love and support more than ever before. Try to nurture yourselves, give yourselves little treats, no matter how small – anything to make life a little easier or more comfortable. Take care of yourself physically – try to eat properly, to rest and sleep. Many of us have found it very difficult to sleep for a long time after our child's death – Sonya and Chris sought the help of their GP who recommended a mild antihistamine tablet (as it is non addictive and is out of the body's system after 12 hours so doesn't leave you feeling groggy the next day) and say it really helped.

Divert your energy
You may suddenly feel that although you have a lot of free time on your hands, your life no longer has meaning or purpose. One mother would often just stay in bed and spend her energy crying. With nothing to do, it can be all too easy to fall into what she calls a "spiral of sorrow", leaving you exhausted from crying and heartache. Falling into a lethargy of despair could be damaging to you physically as well as psychologically, if left unchecked. It may then be a good idea to divert this energy elsewhere. Many of the parents in our network have found great comfort from volunteering at places like a hospice or charity. Go window-shopping or to the museum or (if you feel up to it) to your child's favourite park. If you can muster the energy, it can also be very beneficial to be physically active – many parents have found running, or long early morning walks therapeutic – this may have the added benefit of reducing insomnia. Many people feel that by pouring their energy into physical activity, particularly if it helps others, they are helping to expel their own emotional pain.

Memorials – remembering with love
Memorials provide an invaluable way of staying connected with your child, of acknowledging them and remembering them with love. Memorials can be private or public, and have many forms of expression. Max's family have a bench at the Singapore Zoo, at one of his favourite exhibits (the chimpanzees)

16

with a small plaque with his photo, and their friends at home in the UK planted a tree for him. Some parents have named a star after their child. A father made a CD with special music and photos; another planted a fragrant white flowering bush in the front of their house. An uncle placed a memorial plaque with his niece's name in a new church in London, and her aunt planted a tree for her in Scotland; friends raised money for a new incubator at the NICU where she died. Another friend has written a cookery book with her daughter's favourite recipes. Some parents have set up websites with their children's stories and pictures; others make a donation to a different charity every year on their child's birthday to honour their child's life and the goodness he would have brought. We all keep favourite framed photos.

Friends can also help with memorials. A few months after one child died his tennis group organised a special tournament in his honour, and made a beautifully engraved cup in his name as the trophy. This also allowed all his friends to join in and remember him together.

Talk about him, tell your story
Most of us will find it immensely difficult to talk about our child's death, particularly in the early weeks and months. But it can be very therapeutic.

> *"It took me a while, but I now believe that telling my story about her death helped me manage the reality of my loss. The repetition at first left me miserable, but the more I told my story, the stronger I felt. I am still heartbroken every time I relate it, but not in despair. And I would mention her name if it comes up which may sometimes surprise people. I remember replying to a question "I have three kids – two boys and an angel". I felt good that I did not deny having three children."*
>
> *Val*

Many people, friends and acquaintances and maybe even relatives, might be afraid that if they mention your child's name that it will cause you even more pain. It can help you as well as others to let those around you know that it is OK to speak of your child – that remembering your child is painful, but not as painful as NOT remembering your child. Others will be put at ease by your instruction, because they also do not know what to do or say to help you.

Help siblings to remember without fear
One of the most difficult parts of dealing with your grief for your lost child is

17

to try to explain things to surviving siblings, and to help them to understand what death means whilst not frightening them. One mother talked of how difficult it has been to try to protect her other child from her own pain, putting on a "brave face" when all she wanted to do was collapse in tears. She and her husband worry that he has had to mature early. Another bereaved mother talks of how they make visiting the grave a family outing and also visit nearby farms. One mother always talks to her two-year-old daughter about her special baby brother – every night before she goes to sleep she goes to look at the stars and says she's saying "Good Night" to her brother.

Even with younger children, it can be a challenge – when Max died, his brother Lukas was only four months old, so his mother didn't worry in the same way about putting on a brave face for him, and could cry openly. But he quite obviously picked up on her sorrow and on the changed world that he lived in. She will never forget the look of delight and recognition on his face the day they saw a friends' son (who looked a lot like Max and was around his age) about a month after Max's death. Now, nearly three years on, Max is an important part of Luka's life:

> "We talk about him, look at his pictures and videos of him. Lukas doesn't yet have a mature understanding of what death means, but he does know that he has a brother who is dead, whom we still love and miss, who can't ever come back, and that we're sad about that. I believe that it's very important to talk openly about Max to Lukas and to my younger children – I want them to grow up with a slowly deepening understanding, and never to remember the moment they were first told about their dead brother."
>
> **Sonya**

Siblings keep the continuity

You may have lost your only child now without knowing if you will have another; you may have gone through fertility treatment or feel that time is against you. Or you may already have other children. Whatever the circumstances, it may be helpful to allow some continuity to help in your grief process. Keep some of his things with you for his siblings (present and future). You would be amazed how a simple object can connect you to your lost child. Some parents who have no other children have kept many of their child's favourite toys and clothes with the hope of having other children in the future.

18

One mother kept a small trunk of her child's special toys, shoes, clothes, books and artwork, as well as his birth and death announcements. She plans that her other children will in time be allowed to choose what they would like to keep themselves from his trunk.

But remember that you must pace yourself and go slow if you need to –

"I know that in the first months after Max's death I could not cope with dressing Lukas in Max's clothes or having Max's toys out to play with, and in fact I found it far easier to make things as different as possible – but in time, all the boxes of Max's clothes and toys have come out, and his younger brothers all get to share his things, and now I love it – it helps me to feel that Max is part of the family. I still keep some special things away though, just for me to remember."

Sonya

Couples

You may need time on your own, but allow time together too. Mothers and fathers often grieve quite differently. Some parents found that going away on a trip together, away from "normal life" and the distractions of work and family/friends, really helped them to understand each other's feelings, regrets, hopes and fears.

"We talked and discussed each other's needs and raised the difficult question of whether we would have another child. We found it important to plan our days and weeks together, to be accommodating with each other, and to draw strength from each other. One thing I am always grateful to my husband for was his tact in telling me when I should stop wallowing in my grief. "OK, enough for the day" he would say jokingly, or, "She's watching...she wouldn't want to see you like this." We would then go for a walk, and it made us both feel better."

Val

Use resources

There are many excellent books on grief.

When we could finally force ourselves to venture out into the world we went to scour bookshops for books that might help. I found reading these books hugely therapeutic – I could identify with so much and realised that I was not alone in this frightening

19

new world, that there were many others who had walked this rocky path before and survived, who had felt all the heart wrenching things that I was feeling. In the many, many long lonely hours late at night when we couldn't sleep, I would read chapter after chapter of these books aloud to my husband.

Sonya

We have also found support through the many excellent websites on the internet, particularly reading other bereaved parents' accounts of their own experiences. Some of us have made good friends through these sites and their organisations. (CBC's website at www.childbereavement.org.uk has a discussion forum for families to share experiences and support each other). Parents talk of the comfort they found from realising that other people had "survived" their losses and were coping in various ways: These bereaved parents bear testimony to the saying "life goes on", and that it is possible to find new routines, develop new interests, engage in new activities and be happy again eventually. It seems almost impossible to imagine this in the initial weeks/months/years of your loss, but it is important to try not to lose hope.

Religion/spirituality
Parents who have a religious faith have often found that is has given them enormous strength - and some say that they do not think they could have survived without it. Others have turned away from their faith, feeling "let down" by God. Some have turned away in anger only to turn back to find comfort once again. Some parents have felt that their faith in a loving God and in an afterlife gives them hope - most importantly, hope that their child is in a happy place, and that they will be reunited once again after their own death. Religious rituals have been enormously comforting to some parents. And parents who might not have any religious faith have found comfort in spirituality, believing that their child's soul survives and that there is a deeper meaning behind their child's death.

Tiny steps
So give yourself time, allow yourself to "go with the flow", and don't set yourself great expectations of how you "ought" to be facing the world. Take tiny steps as you move through this unfamiliar new world, congratulating yourself (and your partner) for just getting out of bed and getting through another day, and not giving up and hiding in a darkened room.

You will never "get over it"

Remember, you never "get over" this loss. You only learn, ever so slowly, to live with it. Many other people will be expecting you to move forward at an astonishing rate of recovery. Be kind, gentle and patient with yourself while your broken heart tries to learn to accept the unacceptable – it is by nature a very slow process, full of setbacks and challenges.

Sonya Szpojnarowicz
President, Child Bereavement Support (Singapore)

Untitled

As I look up to the sky
I really wonder why
We had to let you go.

But I know where you are
When I look out for
And see your shining star.

There you are, and there you'll stay
Shining in the milky way
Far, far out of reach.

If I could have had a few last words
Speech would have left me like a flight of birds.
I wouldn't have known what to say.

You'll always have a place, a part
Deep inside my troubled heart
Where you'll never leave.

Jessie Opio
Sonya's god-daughter (aged 12 years)

21

Sebastian
Gabriel Beckley

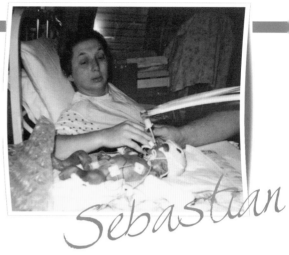

26 September 2000 –
9 October 2000

Sebastian

I became pregnant after trying for sixteen months. Everything progressed normally until the 20 week scan which showed big gaps in the baby's kidneys.

This increased the chances of the baby having Down's Syndrome but the results an amniocentesis test were inconclusive as the doctor had gathered maternal cells with the amniotic fluid. However we discovered our baby was a boy with a kidney problem and a low-lying placenta. I was a first time mother aged 35/6 and started to panic, "Am I too old? What have I done to deserve this?"

When I was 24 weeks, I started to leak pink water at work. I rang my doctor who said she could do a test but there was a risk of it causing an infection, so she told me to pop by the surgery and she would give me a letter and go straight to the hospital. When we got there it was so busy my Mum and I waited for seven hours, standing for most of that time, to see a doctor. A swab was taken, which showed I was leaking amniotic fluid. They needed to find me a bed and phoned Peterborough, Exeter, Southampton and Hillingdon, but none had a free incubator for the baby. Eventually, a bed was found for me; I was pumped full of drugs on the antenatal ward and told not to get out of bed for the duration of the pregnancy.

My husband was in Singapore on business. I phoned him and said I was in hospital but was fine and would be out soon, just so that he didn't worry while he was away! Mum came to spend each day with me. A week later, I developed backache so was given pethidine. The consultant asked if I was having contractions but I didn't know what they felt like as I had never given birth before. He said, "You have lost the plug and you are just leaking fluid.

You are making enough to keep the baby alive but if you go into labour we are in trouble". About midnight, I found I was bleeding heavily. I pressed the panic button and was wheeled straight into the labour ward. My husband had come back by now and was called to the hospital.

I was in labour and 25 weeks pregnant with a baby reckoned to be the weight of a 28-week old baby. There was no bed for the baby and they were talking about sending him to Peterborough. The midwife said, "You're only three centimetres dilated so you have nothing to worry about". They thought the birth would take hours and I should eat something, but when I had some toast I threw it straight up; it was only then that they realised I was in the late stages of labour. A doctor came and examined me and realised he was feeling the baby's legs; he was breech. I had to sign my consent for an epidural and a caesarean. In the strangest of coincidences, I discovered I had met the anaesthetist on a sailing holiday and we talked about that while she was sticking the epidural in my back. I was shaking like a leaf but the midwife was fabulous. I was taken into theatre where I could see everything reflected in the lights. A nurse came in with an emergency incubator looking very worried. They cut me open and pulled the baby out. While I was stitched up they weighed him - two pounds two ounces, a good weight for a 25 week baby. As he cried his lungs haemorrhaged, coughing up a lot of blood. They took him straight to SCBU and I didn't see him for a couple of hours.

When I did get there, the nurse took a photograph of us – he was the length from my elbow to my middle finger. I wish we had taken foot and hand casts. He had lots of lines all over him, oxygen and monitors for his heart, lungs and kidneys. He was covered in bubble wrap under a UV light to warm him. He was flaying and kicking his arms and legs about and they told me to put my hand on him to calm him down. The staff were highly trained and very sympathetic to us. I stayed on the antenatal ward as I needed to be close; this was better because I didn't want to be with people who had given birth, but I also felt I had a right to be on the post natal ward. It all felt a bit of a blur and I felt physically and emotionally numb – there was far too much to take in, it was like a rollercoaster. I just went through the motions and was guided by the staff. The hardest thing to deal with was the consultant Paediatrician telling us the next day at 11pm, "the next 24 hours will be the hardest – if he makes it through the night, then he has a chance".

A week after my c-section (and having been discharged from hospital) I begged the GP to let me drive so that I could get to the hospital by car; the bus took too long and was too painful and I felt I could no longer ask my neighbours for out-of-the way lifts to Slough.

The following two weeks were a living rollercoaster; he had put weight on and lost it, he came off oxygen and went back on it. I was expressing milk to feed him (one fluid ounce every hour) and spending as much of the day in hospital as I could; there were no parent rooms available for me. His lungs had developed scar tissue from the ventilator and his kidneys were not working – he was still not strong enough. One evening when we visited him in SCBU after a night out at the cinema, we spoke with the staff and they asked us to stay the night. We had to go home and collect some night things. All the way home I knew what was going to come next – I knew this meant he wasn't going to last the night. The duty vicar came and christened him and gave him a teddy: it was around midnight. It was agreed that they would take him off the ventilator as it was doing more harm than good. We knew then for sure that he would die. He was put in our arms and one by one the lines were pulled out. I don't know whose arms he died in – it was about 3am. He was put in a cot and given his teddy. The nurse took lots of Polaroid photos of him, hand and footprints, plus a small lock of his hair.

After he died we went home and fell asleep on the sofas. I don't think Carl could deal with it. We also had to decide about the post mortem and organ donation. I am in favour of organ donation but when your baby is only two weeks old the thought of them taking any part of him is too much. We agreed to a partial post mortem and biopsies of his lungs and kidneys and these were sent off to Oxford. The main cause of death was found to be severe scarring changes in his lungs caused by the ventilator, plus the dilated kidney problem diagnosed on the 20 week scan.

At the funeral I was still wearing maternity clothes. We had the top layer of our wedding cake re-iced; it was meant to be for the christening. The funeral directors were brilliant, friendly rather than austere, nothing was too much trouble and it was all done with the utmost respect. We didn't want a hearse – the coffin was far too small – and we didn't want a white coffin. Choosing a coffin is something you think you will never have to do for your child. We want to be cremated so we chose that for him too. We didn't want to cast the ashes in the Memorial Garden as they would get dug in, blown away or washed away with the weather. There is a cemetery at the bottom of the garden and it is nicely kept. We chose a plot next to some nuns big enough for four of us. Married two years and already we'd bought a family plot! However there is something deeply satisfying about it. Sebastian is there so at the end of our days we will all be together. Somehow, that is really comforting.

The hardest thing was choosing the gravestone and inscription – he couldn't have an unmarked grave:

'Our son, so beautiful, he could not stay for long'

It might have been easier if medical science had not been there to keep a child alive who otherwise would have died. There would have been no rollercoaster, no false hope, no 'ifs', 'buts' or 'maybes'. Born, lived a few hours, died, because he was born too early.

Grieving was like being in a cocoon – no one came to see me. At first I stayed in bed and eventually I made it out of the bedroom into other parts of the house. Weeks later I made it out of the house but I was avoided like the plague. Someone who had a baby born at the time Sebastian should have been born crossed the road to avoid me. Two neighbours empathised with me – one had had a terrible pregnancy and birth and the other a premature baby 20 years ago. It hurt too much to associate with people who had children. I stopped reading newspapers and watching the news because there was always a dead or premature baby mentioned.

On my birthday in December I phoned my doctor in floods of tears. Although she was really supportive she couldn't give me any help that day as she was on a half day and picking her mother up for Christmas, so she sent the duty doctor round. He turned up with the nurse and sat in my lounge urging me not to do anything stupid! I was incensed! There was no way I was going to do anything stupid; my son had died, it was my birthday and I was miserable, NOT suicidal! The hospital had recommended a counsellor, so I dug out the number and made an appointment for the New Year. I saw her for 18 months – she was brilliant. Your mind gets really full of things like 'could I have done anything different? Is there anything in my past I have done to deserve this?' It was not just about the baby but also about me and my feelings and how other people reacted to me. I had to realise people grieve in different ways. I tried talking to my mum about Sebastian but she couldn't cope with it because she was hurting too – she had lost a grandchild and her daughter was in deep pain.

I had to go back to see the consultant to determine why I had gone into premature labour but found having to sit waiting in the antenatal clinic deeply disturbing. One possibility was that I had an incompetent cervix and next time they would need to stitch up the cervix.

I went back to work at the end of my maternity leave which was deeply hideous. Two managers' wives gave birth while I was in hospital. I understand now that the personnel manager, while not knowing what to say to me, was trying to convince me not to go back to work. After being back at work a week and now receiving bereavement counselling, I was sacked; however I took legal action against the company and was compensated.

After a series of tests and consultations, my consultant urged me to get pregnant again – one to aid the healing process and two because my tubes were narrowing limiting my chances of becoming pregnant again. I felt fatalistic with the second pregnancy – it was like nothing could touch me. If God was going to take this baby away from me I would go 'up there' and give Him a rollicking! Every week was a milestone and I saw the consultant every two weeks. At the scan, which was nerve-wracking, we found out the baby was a girl. If it had been a boy I don't know how I would have coped as I felt I would always relate back to Sebastian.

When Saskia was born I found it hard to attach myself to her. I was very strict about sterilising and feeding and so on but was happy for her to sit in her bouncy chair – I couldn't hold the child the entire time. I wasn't sure how long she would stay and felt detached. I wasn't going to let this little being control my feelings either. She is and always will be an only child. My main problem with her was that she slept through from 12 days old, but whenever I looked in on her I saw a dead baby. In the darkness her eyes were black and hollow, the hall light giving a faint ethereal glow on her skin. Every night I felt bereft, she was with me during the day, but gone to me at night. She's gorgeous and we tell each other we love each other all the time. Saskia, now 5, knows she has a dead brother who is with the angels.

Various "first" milestones are hard – birthdays, Christmas and Mother's day, in particular, was vile. I still remember the pain buying the cards. It took me three attempts to buy Mother's Day cards and I was in floods of tears each time. Every other bugger gets a mother's day card except you; you have had a child, but he is dead, so there is no child to prove that you are a mother, but you are still expected to go to the shops and get one for your mother and mother-in-law at great emotional cost because you know the consequences if you don't send one. No one phones to say, "How are you feeling today?" Even Carl didn't. I learnt quickly that his grief is very different to mine. He just bottles it up and it comes out in floods every so often. I haven't spoken to my sister since she said "time is a great healer' and "you'll get over it". I wanted people to acknowledge that I am a parent. I always say I have two children rather than one; the first died when he was 2 weeks old. I am the proud mother of two, but only one child is living. I hated the expression "I am sorry for your loss". I didn't lose him or leave him behind in the supermarket. I am always honest about his life and untimely death.

Death is a great leveller – it is imminent, we will all die sometime. People expect you to cope, have a stiff upper lip etc, but that is not the case; nor is it always possible. I have learnt to ask for help when I need it, to say, "Today isn't a good day. I'm dwelling on it too much; can I come over and have a chat?"

After a death you live in a different way and start doing things you have always meant to do. It still hurts every single day. For me it is like stubbing your toe; it still hurts, but you don't cry every time. There are times when it comes and smacks you in the face such as if you hear a song from the funeral. It always comes out of the blue and you have to deal with it. I am lucky in some respects; I never got to the walking/talking phase with Sebastian so there are no milestones or comparisons to make. There are no firsts apart from him holding my finger; he never called me mummy and the only time I got to hold him was when he was dying. It takes a long time for your feelings to come to some semblance of order. I was numb for a very long time but at some stage you come to terms with your grief and you manage it the way it suits you, which is not the way others might manage theirs. Grief is very personal; it is like your fingerprint – it is your grief and it is a unique experience.

Fiona Beckley

Billie Eve Buckley

24 December 2000 – 4 April 2001

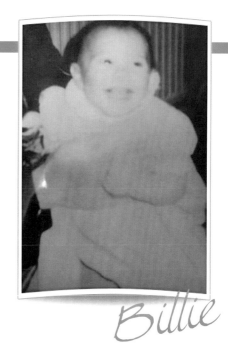

Billie

When we found out we were pregnant we were over the moon about adding another member to our large family, but we were also apprehensive about telling the other 6 children. My partner and I had known each other for several years. I had two children then aged 12 and 17 and he had four aged 13, 12, 10 and 7; their mother had tragically died when the youngest had been 2.

So it was with excitement and trepidation that we were having a child to cement our two families together. Once told, the majority of the children were fine, busy talking about names and what sex the baby would be, whose room it would sleep in, what it would look like etc, whilst the others only began to get excited as the pregnancy progressed.

I loved being pregnant and although we were still in the middle of extending our house to accommodate the family (with all that that entails....) I was slightly worried as I was an 'older mum' at the ripe old age of 37! We had picked out two names for the baby – Tom and Tilly – sensibly one of each sex! So my bump became known affectionately as 'Tom-Tilly'. I tried to include all the children with the preparations for the new baby and it was generally successful.

Tom-Tilly's due date was Christmas Day, and that had caused a stir in our household as it would mean that this would be the first year we had to stay home for Christmas instead of going on our annual two week holiday. However, the promise of TVs and the pick of presents helped to ease the lack of sunshine. I had been early with the Christmas preparations so that all would run smoothly on the day if I was to be in hospital.

And so came Christmas Eve, and the making of the mince pies, when my waters broke. We quickly got to hospital as I was a fast deliverer (5hrs and 2hrs previously) and we weren't disappointed when an hour and 15 minutes later our little baby girl came into the world. She was perfect... a brown haired, blue eyed, olive skinned beauty.

Being born at Christmas time is quite surreal as it reminds you of that other special person born on Christmas Day, and for me she was truly like my own special gift from God. But being born on Christmas Eve and knowing there are six other children not only waiting at home for their new sibling to arrive, but also waiting for 'The Big Day' did put a strain on me to go home sooner rather than later. So with that thought, we decided that if all was well with the two of us, we would take our special Christmas present home to share with the rest of the family. We were discharged from hospital and as we adults were starving we even had time to order a curry on the way home!! In fact we got the delivery guy to take a photograph of all 9 of us and he always enquired after her and wanted to have a hold of her when he came subsequently.

During those early days I did miss not having the 'our' time that I would have had for just me and Tom-Tilly if I had stayed in hospital. But I told myself it was for the good of the family, and anyway they would all be back to school soon so I would have time with her then. We decided to call her Billie, as she didn't look like a Tilly, and Eve for the obvious reason and after her paternal grandmother. But her original name stuck in the form of a nickname, hence she was known as Billie Tom-Tilly.

She wasn't an easy baby, she seemed to be always crying and found it difficult to settle, but I thought she's actually come into quite a busy household with lots of willing and wanting hands. After school each day everyone had to have equal holding time and of course, I did find that quite difficult too as the needs of Billie had to come first and this wasn't always taken into consideration (Well, they were only children themselves) She worried me as well as she would never sleep on her front, only being content with sleeping on her back. I had had two children before and the 'guidelines' had changed for each child – sleeping on their side was preferred with the first and then on their back with the second – so with discussions with the health visitor we decided that it was best for her and for my sanity that she slept how she was obviously comfortable.

On 4th April (two days before Good Friday), Billie went to her first birthday party. I bought her a new dress with matching pants (you know the ones that hide that big bulk of a nappy!) She was laughing and smiling, it was just like any other day. We left the party and went home. The children came home, and after a long day I was tired so decided that I would bath her in the morning. I got her ready for bed, fed her, gave her her nightly cuddle and then passed her to Dad, whilst I watched something on the TV. Sadly I fell asleep and was only woken when Dad was running up the stairs shouting; it was about 2am in the morning.

She was limp when I held her, but she was still warm. I don't know how it all happened, but suddenly everyone was awake, I was giving mouth to mouth, someone else was on the phone, people were crying and then the ambulance came. Her Dad handled it from then on in; I was trying to make tea for everyone. I was praying she would be ok, even accepting that she may have some sort of brain damage or something. It didn't really matter; I just wanted her to be with me. I even thought I heard her crying and ran to the bottom of the stairs clinging onto my eldest daughter in all hope, but sadly it was not to be.

I held her for ages stroking her hair, kissing her face and rocking her back and forth. The worst was to come with the police; the questions, taking her clothes off to inspect her - INSPECT what? - taking away her clothes and bottle from an earlier feed. What the hell did they think we did? The shock was only spared by my body shutting down and going into autopilot. It was becoming light; the day was starting, cars moving, people going to work. How could they? My brain was screaming didn't they know what was happening? Why hadn't everything else stopped like it just had for me?

The next few months are a bit of a blur for me. I was sedated, had a breakdown and began to find it all too difficult; remember there were 8 others to try and support as well. My partner blamed himself as he had let her fall asleep and ironically she was on her tummy when she died, the 'government recommended way' at the time.

It's been seven years since she died and Christmas and Easter have never been the same for me. How can it be? Everyone who's lost someone has an anniversary of course, but mine are always surrounded by the whole Christian world talking about Christmas, Easter and being happy. Sadly our extended family has now split up, but I take some solace in the fact that I have my own little Jesus born on Christmas Eve and taken the day before Good Friday.

Billie Eve Buckley, taken to sleep with the angels, seeing things we've yet to discover.... missing you with each passing day.

All my love Mummy X

Debbie Gay

Billie, my sister, the angel in my life

Billie was like my child that I could give back when I needed to go out, go to sleep, go to college etc. I would come home from college or work and wonder what the little lump was laying on my bed, all curled up like a little ball. As my room was downstairs it was used as a little day nursery for the little cheeky girl when she had dropped off.

In the early afternoon when I would come home from college I would sit and play with her until the others came home. I had more free time during the day so our relationship was very strong. When she was crying, sick or needed feeding and mum was tired or busy with the others I would take her into my room, where it was familiar surroundings, and we would watch TV. She would watch me get ready to go out or I would sit and play silly games with her.

On a Sunday when we needed the morning milk or a paper, I would pack up the buggy and toddle off to Tesco with her; most of the time she would scream the whole way round the store until you picked her up, but it never stopped me taking her.

When she passed away, it didn't seem real. I had exams at college; I had work to go to; I was so focused on the washing and cleaning that I didn't have time to stop! I just wanted to be so exhausted that I didn't think about it. As soon as I would stop or let my mind wander, I would feel the hurt of not seeing her

31

in my room, not feeding her the bottle, not having our daytime bonding sessions, not going to get the Sunday paper down at Tesco's. Suddenly I was wandering round Tesco with no buggy and no Billie; it didn't feel right.

The hardest part of losing Billie was the upset and pain it caused my mum. We had had our ups and downs as mothers and teenage daughters do, but this was just awful! She had a nervous breakdown and I felt I was the only person who could bring her back to some sort of 'normality' but at 17 it was difficult. I had to take her to the doctor's, get her out of bed, see her on continuous meltdown; it was almost like we had lost her too.

Luckily Billie must have heard my prayers as slowly but surely Mum began to rebuild her life, and the path it has led her down is becoming better and better. She went on to have our little treasure Alfie, who I can't imagine life without. He is one of the best things to come out of this. He has enough character, cheek and flair for life for Billie and all the other fallen angels put together.

I was and still am very sad to have lost her, my little Angel, but I take solace in the fact that she was taken whilst sleeping in the arms of her Dad.

Natasha Gay

The best and most beautiful things in the world cannot be seen or even touched.

They must be felt within the heart.

Helen Keller

Tom Clabburn

27 November 1992 –
5 October 2007

Tom

Today should have been my son's 15th birthday. Instead I am writing about life after Tom. Tom died in his sleep in October this year of an undiagnosed heart-related condition. He had been fit, active, healthy, doing well at school, bright and happy. We were not, in any way, prepared.

This is not about my wife, Claire, or my daughter, Ellen. Other than saying that they will always be everything to me, their story is for them. This is about me and Tom. It is about the living and the dead. For at this moment, the two are wrapped around each other in an embrace that is tight and total and painful. I would not have it any other way.

The event that I most dreaded has happened and there are no words to describe how I feel. That, though, has never defeated any hack worth their salt. So here goes.

How do I feel? It's like a tsunami of the soul, a huge destructive overwhelming force that leaves nothing good in its wake and whose ripples surge outwards to touch all those who are near you. Life's landscape changes irrevocably, yet the painfully familiar remains as a reminder of what was. Somehow, in all the devastation, there are tiny patches of upland on which to rebuild. Not quickly, not easily, but you can rebuild. I cling to that thought.

I can no longer control tears, sadness, anger. A word, a gesture, a sound, a fragment of a memory that spins off to replay endlessly, anything and everything can trigger the most abrupt change. At its worst, it is a physical event, a spasm of bleakness, a feeling of sickness deep in my gut. At its best, even in the midst of all this, there is laughter too, often centred on my joker son.

33

Laughter, of course, is no longer straightforward. Happiness and sadness co-exist in the same moment, cradling the same memory in a way I never thought possible. Boundaries no longer matter. Suddenly, every story about someone who has lost a child, whatever the age of parent and whether by bomb or bullet, accident or ill-health, in this country or elsewhere, takes on a different complexion. Where once I could feel only sympathy, now, to a degree, I can empathise. I have a link. I, like all those others, am part of a club I never wanted to join. There are no rules on how I make use of my membership, no handy guides. It's just me.

If you're living, as I do in London, or any part of the affluent West, you "know" that children do not die before their parents. My Mum died in 2005 and my Dad in 2006. They were of the wartime generation, an evacuee and a Normandy veteran, straight out of the school of hard knocks. I grieved long and hard for what I'd lost. Yet they were old and Tom was young. Their deaths were the natural order. His was not.

But children do die. Although the specific cause of Tom's death is comparatively rare, the fact of his passing is not. As a parent, I mostly chose to stay away from this inconvenient fact on the basis that if I thought too hard about such things, I wouldn't be capable of much else. It wasn't something I wanted to think about.

In the immediate days after Tom's death, shock took over. Shock helps. Shock protects. On the afternoon of Tom's funeral, I drank more than I've done in decades, by my standards enough to sink a battleship. I didn't feel a thing. Next day I had no hangover, total recall and an overpowering sense of "What next?" The rest of my life was the answer.

Shock has been replaced over the following weeks by endless questions revolving around "What if?" and "If only?" It is draining. I struggle to get out of bed. I make myself do so because it is only by physically putting one foot in front of the other, walking and talking with my wife, that I can start another day and head to work. I try to confront as much as I can, go to the places he and I used to go, watch what we used to watch together. It is a battle and I am fighting it as aggressively as I am able.

Anger, I'm told, is natural at this time. Ever eaten a fried egg in a fury? Tom liked fried eggs. So do I, yet I wasn't sure I could face one. The first time I did, I did so because I am not going to give up what he or I enjoyed. I forced it down. It was a small victory. So anger can help, it can help me to push back against fate, to tell myself that however low I go, I will not stay down, I will look the world in the eye and to hell with anyone who doesn't want to look back.

I can honestly say I'm not angry at any individual. There is nobody to blame for Tom's death, for which I am grateful. My rage is at the unfairness and it means I do not always cope as I should. Sadness, though, is the predominant emotion and I have my own strategies for self-preservation. I've gone to counselling for the first time and found it useful.

I've always enjoyed a beer, now I've cut right back because just one occasion so far was enough to show that grief and too much alcohol doesn't work for me. So no booze and a shrink is the answer? Whatever works is the answer.

Being prepared is also part of my self-preservation. The perfectly normal question, "How are you?" can throw me completely. Now, I have my honest, autopilot replies of "It's hour by hour" or "Ask me in 10 years". If you're really lucky, I might give both replies, or I might take you through things. I simply don't know.

What can people say? Therein is a huge issue. Not only is there no guidebook for me – well, there are a few and I'm reading them – there are also no guides for friends or colleagues. People are unsure about the approach to take. Do they say too little or too much? Do they acknowledge or do they ignore? Do they talk about their children or not?

It's therefore not only about when I am ready to speak to people; it's also about when they are ready to speak to me. I try to keep in mind that, even when I've been asked a truly insensitive question or had to listen to someone muse on how they might feel in similar circumstances, they're trying to reach out. We're all walking on eggshells which break without warning.

The absolute truth about how I feel remains within me, within my family and with my closest friends. Upon them rests the dubious distinction of me admitting if I feel terrible. I'm not going to dwell on it any more than I can help, neither am I going to say I'm okay if I'm not. If they feel terrible, they tell me, or at least they claim they do. I don't trust another person's protective instincts. I can't see any other way other than such honesty if relationships are not to fracture under the weight of tip-toeing around the big bastard elephant in the corner.

Our friends are mourning our son and trying to support us. They are doing a magnificent job and I do not under-estimate the cost. This is just about the most public way I know of saying: "Thank you – and look out for yourselves." I acknowledge, too, that so many people have shown a huge generosity of spirit, cooking food, running errands, putting time and effort into showing they care.

Tom's own friends have posted all sorts of tributes on the net and I take strength from what I see. Type in "RIP Tom" on You Tube and my son appears alongside others who have died too young. There, that link, again.

The kindness of strangers is also remarkable. People have shared what they had previously kept hidden – their own similar experiences as parents or siblings. One person confided that they were an alcoholic in an effort to steer me clear of seeing drink as the answer. I want to thank them all: from the bloke who installed our boiler to the builders working on our house; from the people at Cardiac Risk in the Young (www.c-r-y.org.uk), to the journalist Matthew Engel (www.laurieengelfund.org) who responded to my wife's ad hoc letter.

After so many words, I think what I've written is an aide memoire. I've loved my son and daughter equally, learned from both equally and will continue to both love and learn from them. I'm not looking for "closure", I'm looking for Tom to stay with me in a way that allows me to smile as well as mourn.

It's a different journey from the one I wanted, no doubt with many missed turnings and steep hills along the way. However, it is a journey that I hope I – and we as a family – will continue to go on. And we will make it.

Paul Clabburn   **© BBC News Website**

Lucy S.O. Empson

14 June 1972 - 12 October 2002

It isn't for the moment that you are struck that you need courage,
but for the long uphill climb back to sanity and faith and security
Anne Morrow Lindbergh

in 'Forgiveness and Other Acts of Love' by Stephanie Dowrick

I told you not to go. No, that's not quite correct. I said I wouldn't go to the other side of the world when everything in my life was so perfect, as it was with you at the time. You had your own flat, a new car, you had just been promoted to a dream job in the music industry and your 3-year-old niece and nephew of 6 months simply adored you and you them. Finally, there was the love of your life, Darryl, with whom you had just got back together after a three month break - he had just moved in with you, days before you left for Bali.

Lucy, you always told me I was intuitive and so it proved to be. There was an edginess about me when you told me you were thinking of going to Bali with your dear friend, Emma, for your much-loved holiday in the sun. This was to be your last 'girlie' holiday before you settled down with Darryl and you insisted it was going to be a good one. I suggested the Caribbean, being not so far to travel, but you completely rejected that idea. Your heart was set on Bali, wasn't it Lucy?

You booked your holiday over the Internet some weeks before you went. I still have the emails you and Emma sent back and forth to one another while you were at work, getting more and more excited as your dream holiday got closer. For two 30-year-old marketing managers it just had to be a two-day shopping spree in Singapore first before soaking up the sun at a luxury hotel in Bali.

Dad and I took you both to Heathrow on Tuesday 8 October. Even at your age, Lucy, I couldn't resist saying to you to keep together at all times – it's just what mothers do! You always understood the love and anxiety I felt for you, especially at times such as these. I'm sure your understanding was borne of the love you had for me in return. We were mother and daughter, best friends, kindred spirits all rolled into one, weren't we, Lucy?

When you said goodbye to Dad I marvelled at the length of time you cuddled him. When it was my turn to kiss you goodbye for the last time I was yet again in awe of your small face, the softness of your cheeks and the wonder of your beauty. And then you were gone.

I knew everything you did during the last few days of your life because of the wonders of text messaging. One of your last messages was to let me know you had landed in Bali and hours later you and Emma lost your lives in the Bali terrorist bombings of October 2002.

You were such a wonderful child, Lucy, born 15 months after we lost our second son, Jeremy, to kidney failure at a month old. I often told you throughout your life the joy your birth brought to us and also to your brother, Gary, who was nearly 4 at the time. Gary couldn't understand how he could welcome his new brother into the world with such excitement and then four weeks later to be robbed of his playmate. Naturally, he wouldn't let you go in the early days of your life and was definitely a 'hands-on' brother, caring for your every need. In return, you were so kind to him from an early age when he suffered bouts of asthma. When invitations had to be cancelled because of his illness you never showed your disappointment to any of us – your only concern was for your brother's health. Everybody dearly loved you because of your happy and unselfish nature.

You adored your school years, excelled at most sports, particularly loved dancing, passed your important school exams and followed your brother to University. We were so proud of you, as we were with Gary. We loved being the parents of you two – you were our lives, and that is all we ever wanted.

38

But life took another tragic turn for us on 12 October 2002. I had missed the early evening news and turned to Ceefax where it said there had been a bomb in Bali. With sheer desperation at my fingertips I sent you a short text message: 'R u OK?' I truly knew at the time you would have returned a message to me immediately, even under the most difficult of circumstances, such was your loyalty to my love of you and your love of me. I prayed for the shrill sound of the text messaging bleeps but they never came and I knew then that you had left me.

And so it is, Lucy, that I have been grieving for 5 years now. Dad and I have happy moments, of course we do, but our life will never be the same without you in it, and you would know that more than anybody, wouldn't you? We spoke about anything and everything, didn't we? We thought we loved you with a passion the day you were born but with every year of your life that followed, the love just grew and grew.

Did you know that I wrote a diary in the immediate aftermath of the bombings and kept it going for three years? You would have been so proud of me, especially when there were days when I was so bereft with grief that all I ever wanted to do was close my eyes on another day. However, I always seemed to find the strength from somewhere (it must have been you!) to complete another A4 page diary entry. It so helped me in the early years to express my grief on paper, keeping a record of all that followed and making a note of people that helped us so magnificently along the way. By the way, Lucy, your close friends continue to keep in touch with us. It gives us such comfort to hear from them.

I know you will also be thrilled to hear news of your dear brother and sister-in-law, Lucy. They moved house to live near us, giving us such strength and support. The family, too, have been wonderful, as have good friends and new ones we have made since. We were assigned an incredible Family Liaison Officer to help us during those early weeks and months. What a truly magnificent service that is! Support also came from the Child Bereavement Charity, a guardian angel coming to us at a time when we were both on our knees with grief, picking us up and giving us the will to fight against the agonising heartache that engulfed us.

Yet with all this tremendous support there was still a powerful need in me for more understanding and information on intense bereavement, so I took myself off to the local library to look for books on the loss of a child. There were many on the loss of a baby, young child or teenager but limited material on the loss of an adult child. So it was that I started grasping for comfort from newspaper cuttings and magazine articles of parents that had lost an older child. The quotes of these parents in the reports confirmed my acute feelings of grief as 'normal'. I also drew comfort from the fact that we were not the only mature parents living in Griefland. Lucy, I remember so well our conversation when we talked about my ambition to write a book one day. You said I should give up my job and fulfil my dream. I responded by saying I would if I had a story to tell. That moment has come back to haunt me, my darling. But who knows, with the help of my diaries and my need to support others in a similar situation, the book you asked me to write could one day be a reality, dedicated to my beautiful daughter. In that book I would tell the world how it is to lose a daughter as precious as you, underlining the complexities of losing an older child.

In closing, my dear Lucy, I speak for Dad as well as myself in telling you that we still miss you as much today as we did in the frantic early days of our grief. Your loss never gets any easier to bear. What does get easier, however, is the way we now conduct ourselves in front of others, although I have to say it has been more of a struggle for me than it has for your dear father. Although we cannot see you, hear you or feel you we love you more and more as the years of your loss advance. You will forever be our beloved daughter till the day we die. We were, indeed, privileged to have had you for 30 glorious years.

Sandra Empson

40

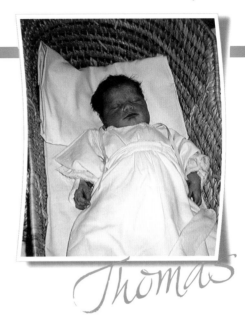

Thomas Henry Fone

20 May 1996 - 21 May 1996

Thomas Henry Fone has been likened to a Mayfly; he lived his whole life in one day.

My husband Mark and my first child, Thomas, was conceived easily and my pregnancy healthy. I ate well, continued to exercise and work as a chartered physiotherapist. Six weeks into my pregnancy I had had a particularly distressing day at work, listening to a Colombian lady who had watched her son being shot dead in front of her. I went to the loo later and found that I had had some bleeding. A scan organised by my GP showed that the foetus was "viable" and all was well.

Then at three months I was caught up in a bank raid! A gun was wielded and we were all told to lie face down on the floor. My emotion turned from disbelief to tears and relief when the robber fled. (As a physiotherapist dealing with patients I have always wondered whether these emotional situations had any influence on the development of our son.) Following a holiday in Antigua, I returned home to attend ante-natal classes at 26 weeks. My tummy was quite enormous compared to the other mothers. I was the only one to experience Braxton Hicks contractions and the midwife felt that I should have another scan.

I happily went along to Chelsea and Westminster Hospital believing that I had a big, healthy baby cooking, but was told that actually the baby had bilateral pleural effusions (fluid on the lungs) and it was confirmed that I had polyhydramnios (extra fluid). A further heart scan showed all was well and that the worst possibility was that the baby could have Down's Syndrome.

41

Mark and I decided that we would not terminate the pregnancy if this were the case, so no further investigations were taken. I was then scanned weekly and the effusions remained static.

My waters broke at 38 weeks and I was transferred to St Mary's Paddington as a special care baby unit or intensive care was needed in case of problems. My labour was long, 30 hours to be precise (my father believes this was because Thomas knew that as soon as he was born his time with us would be up). Thomas was born on Monday 20th May at 12.30pm to our utter joy and exhilaration. He opened his blue eyes to us and gasped but did not cry. He had broad shoulders, a mass of black hair, a well-developed body and a handsome face. He was put on my chest for a brief moment and then taken away with Mark to intensive care. He opened his eyes, smiled and squeezed Mark's fingers on his way. Mark had this overwhelming sense of respect for his first born. Gosh, this is painful to write; the emotions feel as acute today as they were when we had those short, intense moments with Thomas alive.

Thomas was ventilated and hopes were high that all would be well. My parents and sister, Lucy, came up to see me and flowers began arriving. They were unable to see Thomas as the doctors were busy treating him - little did we know that they would never meet their new relative alive. We had no idea that time was so acute and precious; I thought we would all have a lifetime for developing relationships. Sadly, his condition deteriorated as he developed a pneumothorax - a burst lung due to the ventilator. We stroked and kissed him and told him how much we loved him. I just prayed to God that he was to take him if he was going to suffer at all. I did not want him to be kept alive if he would be in any pain or distress. I couldn't believe that this was my son, Thomas, on whom we were looking down. I felt I didn't know him; I knew him well as 'BLOB' - the 'BLOB' who adored classical music, who was an active and strong kicker. The consultant said that as soon as he felt that his brain was being compromised due to a lack of oxygen, then they would not continue with treatment. We agreed with this.

As a Catholic, I wanted him baptised and a priest was called. We stood around Thomas's cot and said the Lord's Prayer and he was christened Thomas Henry. We then both held him in our arms as the ventilator was switched off. The time was 6.30am, the exact time that my mother woke up screaming in agony with severe cramp in her calf (she has never had this before). How powerful is that bond between mother and child?

We were taken to a private room with Thomas and told we could have as much time with him as we needed. The nurse suggested that we bathe him, and put a nappy on him. I was shocked and said, "But he's dead". To this day I am thankful to the nurse for suggesting this. I so remember how gently and delicately I washed him and brushed his hair. I didn't want to hurt him.

As soon as you become pregnant I believe you are a mother and, in most of us, those mothering instincts are instantaneous. I was longing to give my baby his first bath, put a nappy on him, burp him, take him to the supermarket and show him off for the first time.

Mark and I hugged Thomas, each other, cried, howled, smiled, caressed as we grew closer together in our grief. Complete disbelief, a surreal feeling, an out-of-body experience. My parents and my mother-in-law came to the hospital on hearing of his death, and held and hugged their grandson. Such respect emanated from us all. Here was this little fellow, with lots of dark hair and a smile on his face, having done something that none of us had done.

To leave a hospital without one's baby in one's arms must be one of the most forlorn experiences. I stood in the foyer, waiting for Mark to bring round the car, surrounded by flowers and my large belly still in situ. Leaving the hospital was truly heart-wrenching; my heart actually physically ached.

Each morning we would wake with that awful feeling of absolute doom but then be cheered by wonderful letters from friends, family and acquaintances, telling tales that I did not know about their own experiences of grief and pain or just cheering quotes from prose and poetry.

Thomas's coffin was brought home on the day of his funeral. It was so tiny. It was then placed in a funeral car and we drove slowly down our road in Wandsworth with two funeral directors walking with heads bowed in front of the car. Our neighbours came out with looks of bewilderment, not knowing at this point what had happened. I'm afraid we did giggle as it was a most bizarre experience. A griever's prerogative. Mark gave the most moving and uplifting speech in honour of his first born and the day turned into a celebration of Thomas's very short life.

A post mortem showed that Thomas had died of a rare genetic condition called alveolar capillary dysplasia. Weeks later we had further devastating news from a geneticist that the condition is an autosomal recessive condition and that we would have a one-in-four chance of the same thing happening again.

Well, eleven years later, we now have two sons, Freddie, who is 10, and eight-year-old Alexander. We talk about Thomas and he is very much part of our family. The boys know that they have a special guardian angel protecting them.

I have a strong faith which has been sorely tested. I prayed and prayed that all would be well, but this was not to be. I hated God – I blamed him for his death. But in my grief, my main solace was from poetry and prayer. It was when I screamed and hollered to God that I felt more at peace afterwards and I felt his love and sadness, too. It is only when you lose that you truly live and appreciate that life is a journey with its ups and downs. God doesn't orchestrate our lives but he is there to help us through those desolate moments.

Footprints
One night I had a dream.
I dreamed I was walking along a beach with God
and across the sky flashed scenes from my life.
For each scene I noticed two sets of footprints in the sand,
one belonged to me and the other to God.
When the last scene of my life flashed before me
I looked back at the footprints in the sand.
I noticed that at times along the path of life
there was only one set of footprints.
I also noticed that it happened at the very lowest and saddest
times of my life.
This really bothered me and I questioned God about it.
'God, you said that once I decided to follow you
You would walk with me all the way, but I noticed that during
the most troublesome time in my life there is only one set of
footprints.
I don't understand why, in times when I needed you most,
you would leave me?'
God replied, 'My precious, precious child,
I love you and I would never, never leave you
During your times of trials and suffering
when you see only one set of footprints,
it was then that I carried you.'

Anon

44

There were some painful moments after Thomas's death: receiving a postcard, from my brother Nick, who was abroad when Thomas had been born, welcoming his nephew into the world. The first visit to the supermarket without my son; I wanted to have a T-shirt emblazoned with 'I am a mother but my son died' upon it. The midwife who arrived on my first day home, waiting expectantly to see my son; I had to tell her that he had died. Having a bath and watching my milk pour out of my breasts. Having supper out with a group of girlfriends and them showing pictures of their children, and Thomas wasn't mentioned (I know that they didn't want to upset me and as I was on 'good form' they thought they wouldn't mention him). I had brought all my photos of Thomas along as well but never got a chance to show them.

I still get pangs of sadness when I see a mother with three sons. Then I think, could I cope with three lots of filthy rugby kits to wash on a Sunday?!

What have I learnt from the loss of Thomas? I know that I can cope with anything life throws at me. The human spirit has infinite power to cope with the most distressing of experiences. This is backed up time and time again. You make the decision to lie down and die inside, or go on living just as your loved one would wish you to.

I've learnt that it is possible to be 100 per cent happy again; you just have to go through the grieving process the best you can. And go with it; don't suppress your feelings, talk to anyone who will listen; this may be a good friend or a counsellor.

I've learnt that one does not ever get over the loss, but you learn to live with it. TIME is an amazing healer. I am a better, more empathetic physiotherapist for losing Thomas. The loss takes your relationships and friendships onto another, deeper level.

I've learnt that we are all here on earth for a short time; one must try to make the most of it and cherish family and relationships.

> *Dearest Thomas,*
> *We love you and have such high regard for you. You are and shall always be a major player in our family. I feel honoured to have such a precious guardian angel watching over us all. Your brothers talk to you and know that you are protecting them. Watch over us and guide us until we meet again.*
> **All our love Mummy and Daddy xxxxx**

45

Surmise

My son, whose face I never saw
Who could not wait to bless your father's eyes
With wonder, but in such mysterious wise
Slipped from our world bound hard by lust and war
But warm for you with love, in silent awe
We ponder, in a shrouded deep surmise
Your swifter summons to the world that lies
In our own path beyond the self same door.

Was there a need some work there sudden and great
Your work? Or do you there prepare our home
Least we be timid, touched with fear and sin
Will you beside that portal wait,
Who when your father and your mother come
Will take us by the hand and lead us in.

Michael Thwaites

Mark and Clare Fone

Frederick George Arthur Greenwood

19 September 2002

Freddie

On Friday 13th September 2002, twenty one weeks into my first pregnancy, I woke in the middle of the night to discover that my waters had broken. Being my first pregnancy we genuinely did not know what was going on. We went to hospital in Norfolk where I was visiting my Mother, to be told I was OK and just to go to my GP on the Monday.

As soon as my doctor saw me she sent me straight to hospital; God only knows what the doctors were thinking about in Norfolk. The odds were stacked against us, throughout the ordeal I was engulfed in utter despair and disbelief. I was only there a few days before our worst fears were realised. On the 19th September at 10pm I went into spontaneous labour and gave birth to our son Frederick George Arthur Greenwood just ten minutes later. Freddie was 18 weeks premature and was simply too tiny and not developed enough to survive. His birth was and will remain forever the most amazing yet saddest moment of our entire lives. He breathed for only forty five minutes, his little finger tightly gripped to mine. He was our little angel, our perfect little boy, and our hearts were broken beyond repair.

We were so grateful for the bereavement care of the staff at the Chelsea and Westminster: among our most treasured mementoes are the photographs taken by a nurse using a hospital camera. These pictures sit among other family photographs in our sitting room. They are the first things we would take if the house was on fire. When Freddie went into the hospital's chapel of rest, he was blessed by the chaplain. We went in every day till the cremation, and our parents came to share those moments and to see their grandchild.

47

The first few weeks after losing Freddie were horrendous; Will, my mother and the rest of my family were wonderful, but I was numb and not much use to anyone. I didn't want to wake up, I couldn't get out of bed, I was angry at the whole world – myself mostly. I felt nobody could or would ever understand how I felt. I wanted to wear black forever and never open the curtains again. It is an especially vulnerable time for bereaved mothers; your body is telling you physically and emotionally that you are a mother. You are lactating, but you feel in despair and wretched because your lovely baby has not survived. Many hospital workers had no idea what to say; they took my blood pressure and left. Others gave me a hug, sympathised and sat down and talked, sometimes for a long time. These are people I will remember for ever.

Will: *For months, Caro and I thought of Freddie almost every moment. I found a release in rugby, where I was among great friends. During a game or training, I was totally focused. But as soon as the whistle went – even during a 30-second break in play – my mind raced back to my grief.*

It took a very long time and huge amounts of support from friends and family to come to terms with his death. When I eventually managed to go a whole day without crying, I felt I had done something wrong; that I was not mourning Freddie properly. Days turned into weeks, weeks into months, and months into years. It seems unbelievable that it is now five years ago that we had our precious little boy.

The CBC were very supportive, not just for us but for our families also. It's so easy to concentrate on us, the Mummies and Daddies; you tend to forget about the Grannies, Grandpas, sisters, brothers etc. We lived in ignorant bliss that a charity like this even existed, but thank goodness it does.

We feel incredibly lucky to now have Archie who will be four in January and Matilda who will be two in April. We remember Freddie every day but talk about him the most on his birthday. This year I felt Archie was old enough to learn about his big brother. I didn't think he had digested any of it, but heard him chatting to his little friend the other day; *"I've got a brother called Freddie you know, he's not here though, he's in heaven"*. It has taken a long time to get here, but never has such a sad statement made me so happy.

Will: *Freddie had a short life, but he is part of our family. I often think about him when the final whistle goes, and hope he is out there somewhere and proud of his old man.*

Caroline and Will Greenwood

48

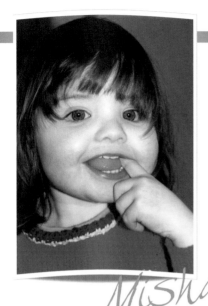

Misha

Natalie

Misha Hannah Griffith

14 November 1995 –
27 November 2002

Natalie India Griffith

20 December 1997 –
8 December 2003

Misha Hannah Griffith was born seven weeks prematurely, on 14th November 1995. Two years later, on 20th December 1997, Misha was joined by her sister Natalie who arrived very suddenly after a much happier birth. Life certainly was good; I had started a new job and we had moved to a larger house in the village of Whitchurch.

However, things took a dramatic turn for the worse in May 1999. We had decided to join friends on a cottage holiday in Port Isaac in Cornwall. The sun was shimmering across the water, the birds were singing and the girls were laughing - what could be more perfect? It took a few seconds for me to realise that Misha had stopped playing and was standing motionless, her eyes flickering, not making a sound. Being a trained nurse, Rachel recognised the signs and confirmed my fears that Misha was fitting. An ambulance was called, but Misha's airway was blocked and she stopped breathing.

49

Fortunately, Rachel's training came into play and Misha was placed in the recovery position. After fitting for several minutes, she went into a deep sleep.

The ambulance took Misha to Truro hospital and, following several hours of tests the doctors confirmed fears of epilepsy. In the subsequent weeks, more fits followed. We were referred to a neurologist at the John Radcliffe Hospital in Oxford and despite months of tests, the doctors were still no closer to an answer. By this time, Misha had started to fall down the stairs and her speech had gradually worsened. On Christmas Eve in 1999, Misha was taken for one last test at the hospital. A skin biopsy was taken and we had to wait over a month for the results.

The New Millennium arrived and with it, many changes. Another daughter, Sophie, arrived on 30th January 2000. A week later came the devastating news that Misha had Late Infantile Batten Disease. Being genetic, Misha's sisters also had to be tested.

There had been no previous cases in our families' history; the odds of us getting together to create the defective gene were about one in a million. Initially suicidal, we soon focused on the needs of the family. The news that Natalie also had the disease - Sophie was clear - was almost too much to comprehend; after all, Natalie was bright, outgoing and intelligent, and had shown no signs of the disease. Maybe the doctors had got it wrong. Unbelievably, the results were confirmed. Natalie started fitting in February 2001. She deteriorated quicker than Misha and her fits were more severe, leaving us feeling totally helpless.

In an effort to come to terms with the impact of the disease on us as a family, we found support in the form of the Batten Disease Family Association, a recently established parent support group. We met other families and children affected by the disease, which helped us to understand the process of the illness, to cope and find ways to give a quality of life to our dying children. We also realised we weren't alone and soon got involved with the BDFA, forming strong friendships along the way.

In September 2001, Rachel and I found we were expecting our fourth child. With concerns that this child could also be affected, we found that the embryo could be tested for Battens. Not wanting to terminate the pregnancy, but also not wanting to bring a child into the world that would suffer in the same way as Misha and Natalie, we were faced with the prospect of having to make some tough decisions. Fortunately, Chorionic Villi tests proved negative and Zak, a healthy boy, was born on 14th May 2002, to his very proud (if extremely emotional) parents.

Helen House Children's Hospice in Oxford proved to be an invaluable sanctuary of solace, rest and peace when we found ourselves unable to cope. It was here that Misha was brought, following a day of uncontrollable fitting, the result of a severe chest infection.

Misha died peacefully in our arms five days after being admitted, on the 27th November 2002, shortly after her seventh birthday.

Natalie was a fighter but sadly she too died just over a year later on 8th December 2003, aged 5, just twelve days before her 6th birthday.

Misha was buried in our village, about half a mile from our house and in the first days, I felt the need to visit the grave each day. I would talk to her and tell her how sorry I was that she had to suffer so much in her short life. Being the first child, she had to endure our training as new parents. When she first started having problems, I was overcome with guilt that we might have caused her some harm. I often asked Misha for forgiveness, but the guilt still lingers. I also felt sorry for her that through no choice of her own she had been given this bitter inheritance and things could have been different if she had come to different parents.

I know for many men, being able to express their grief can be very difficult, but I found that talking through my thoughts and fears was a way of exorcising my grief. I remember on one occasion, when out with 'the boys' for a drink, the conversation seemed fairly superficial. As the evening went by, I got more and more frustrated. No one seemed to notice or acknowledge the fact that I had just buried my daughter and I felt like smashing my glass against the wall and screaming at them. I didn't feel like I fitted in anywhere; I just wanted the world to stop and notice.

Rachel and I dealt with things very differently. The children needed her and she was worried that if she opened the lid to her emotions, it would be impossible for her to put the lid back on and control them. This caused us to grow apart. I felt very isolated, like an onlooker to the situation and the family. As Rach and the family got back to some sort of life, mine seemed to be on hold. My memory, which I had taken for granted, left me. I found myself booking appointments one day for the next, only to have the client ring me

51

and enquire of my whereabouts. Even simple work tasks seemed impossible at that time and I even started to question my sanity. Things fortunately have improved over time.

To try and find some sort of comfort and understanding of what was happening to me, I sought to find an intimacy through sex with Rach. This only led to resentment when Rach wouldn't consent and only enhanced the feeling of isolation. Being a proud male, I thought I would never need counselling, but as the days went by, it became clear that I was on my way to a breakdown. After talking with our doctor, both Rach and I took up individual counselling sessions, provided by social services. However, it became clear after a few sessions that the counsellor had no experience of counselling a parent who had lost a child. I quickly stopped attending and was kicked off the course, with no offer of further counselling sessions. I would definitely recommend specialist bereavement counselling around the time of the loss of a child.

Fortunately, about this time, we had been given the contact details of the Child Bereavement Charity. This was the first time we had talked through the experience together with a third party. We were encouraged to come to the appointments together and, over a cup of coffee, were invited to share... and, as they say, it was emotional! It was clear that there was a deep understanding of where we were coming from. We were encouraged that we had managed well in being so open with the children through the whole process and we left feeling a lot closer than we had done for several weeks.

We met several times and were able to vent our feelings of frustration and anger at one another, helping to destruct the walls that we had built between us. The charity also ran a group for bereaved parents which we attended. Each parent had the opportunity to share in turn their experience of losing their child. The room filled with such raw emotion, you could taste it. I could feel the tears flowing, but a deep sense of acceptance and belonging also emerged. As it got to my turn, the words wouldn't come and I was choked for probably the first time since Misha's death. The experience touched a part of me I hadn't been willing to explore until then and I felt a relief that I could let go of things and feelings I had held onto until that point. The experience left both Rach and I feeling very drained and shattered, but it was the catalyst for us to talk openly and honestly and to find common ground in our grief.

After each of the girl's deaths we also attended a series of bereavement counselling sessions with other parents from Helen House. During these times I was able to share some of my guilt in caring for Misha. We found that making ourselves vulnerable and sharing many common experiences helped to give us strength. We wanted to grieve each child separately as we felt they deserved; at times grief was so intertwined with managing care and daily life. We have also been invited to share our experiences with our church members and a group of professionals at a weekend course run by CBC. We have tried to look outward rather than inward and make the most of every day we have been given with our children as a blessing. We hope our shared experiences will enable others to support other families with similar experiences.

I can't believe where the last years have gone since Misha and Natalie have died, nearly 4 and 5 years ago. I have felt the guilt of not visiting Misha's grave on a regular basis, where I made a promise to myself to go every week. It is here that I find myself talking with Misha and telling her what's happening within the family. I have found myself so busy with my business that I have struggled to find time to spend with the family and I still kick myself for that. I had made a promise that work would take second place, but the reality isn't that easy.

I am learning that for me grief will be something I will live with all my life. Both friends and family struggle to try and make our lives normal again. They tell us that we will get over it and move on. I will never get over losing my daughters, but I will learn to adapt and adjust. The pain has left a scar that will never go away and it will be a part of who I am. I feel very proud to be the father of two girls that have been brave beyond words and who, in their short lives, have touched so many more than they would have done had they lived a 'normal' life without the disease.

I know we will see the girls again, but until then we have to find a purpose to our lives, to make sense of what has happened and to learn all we can through their experience, so that their lives will not have been in vain. In between the deaths of Misha and Natalie, we tried to change some of the circumstances we had found ourselves in with Misha so circumstances were better with Natalie. Now, we spend lots of time and energy supporting the charities that supported us. We use our skills in the areas that we can to try to make a difference as others had done for us.

We also know a need to equip both ourselves and our children with the tools to help them and us cope with the future. Sophie does remember her sisters

53

and loves to talk about the things we all did together, but I'm sure we'll still have many awkward questions to face. Zak has little recollection of Misha and Natalie, but he does love to share in the pictures and videos we made at the time so that we might include him in those experiences. He is mainly concerned about what he missed out on and so asks over and over when we will take him to Disneyland! Through the support that CBC and Helen House have to offer, we aim to provide Sophie and Zak with the tools and skills that will help them to grow into beautiful adults.

Things that help us now are taking time to be together and appreciating time as a family. If we are unable to manage holidays, we take days out and go for picnics. We take time off work to have space and be sad if we want to around the girls' anniversaries and birthdays. We celebrate their birthdays with a cake that Sophie, Zak and their cousins can decorate and we release balloons by their gravesides to say thank you for the gift we had of our gorgeous girls.

Our faith has been our rock in the last years and yet, at the same time, it has been challenged to the highest degree. Our comforts have been in our true friends' faithful and practical support in the hardest times. Our prayers have been for strength to be good and loving parents. Here are a few of the words that have strengthened and supported us....

Psalm 23

1. *The Lord is my shepherd I shall not be in want*
2. *He makes me lie down in green pastures, he leads me beside quiet waters.*
3. *He restores my soul. He guides me in paths of righteousness for his name's sake.*
4. *Even though I walk through the valley of the shadow of death, I will fear no evil for you are with me; your rod and staff they comfort me.*
5. *You prepare a table before me in the presence of my enemies. You anoint my head with oil; my cup overflows.*
6. *Surely goodness and love will follow me all the days of my life, and I will dwell in the house of the Lord for ever.*

(The Bible NIV version)

These words are very familiar, yet strengthening and comforting. The words say that we should walk through the valley of the shadow of death and we believe that this should be so. We should not try to run or jump or crawl through this place.

One step at a time is sometimes all we can manage, but time does move and life does go on without us if we let it. We can rarely manage these times in our lives without help and support. It is a humbling and difficult place to be in need of support, but I would encourage everyone to seek a listening ear and a practical hand. We have found that in the deepest darkest times, our God has been a supporting spiritual and physical presence.

Peter and Rachel Griffith

Song for Nat - by Ed May, December 2003

All that glistens is gold; you're a treasure we know,
Jesus holds you in the palm of his hand.
Tender hearts he holds dear, your soul he draws near.
In his arms you'll find rest, at last.

Chorus
'Cause there's a smile on your face,
That I'd love to embrace.
'Cause I know it's a smile, from God's own.

And all those long years, of crying those tears
Left behind with the memories, that scar.
If I thought that I could, if I knew that God would,
I'd pray to take your place, in this world.

Chorus

No more suffering and pain, in time that's ordained,
By our Lord Jesus, Saviour and lamb.
'Cause he's promised to you, a life made renewed
Your trust and your faith he has called.

Chorus

No more tears shall we cry, Jesus holds you on high,
In a place where he says, you will shine.
We'll be together again, with hugs, kisses and then
Dancin, runnin and jumpin' for joy.

Chorus

55

Hazel Guinn

14 November 1999 –
8 November 2003

Hazel

Life was pretty much fantastic before Hazel died. Summer 2003 was the best summer of my life, I spent the holidays having fun with Hazel who was three and her little sister Shelley, one. I loved my life of looking after the girls and taking Hazel to nursery for her afternoon session every day. I used to often make a point of stopping to think how lucky I was, to appreciate the moments with them before they quickly grew up and left home.

She was a lovely girl, fun and easy going, the nicest person I have ever met. Hazel and I had a fantastic relationship, we loved being together and I thought she would be there for the rest of my life. We shared the same birthday, which I loved, except that I thought it would be a shame when I died that her birthdays would be a bit sad.

One Wednesday in November Hazel had a friend round to play after nursery. She wasn't herself, was rather quiet, and during the night came down with a high temperature and was hallucinating. We called the doctor, who advised us to give Calpol and Nurofen, which we did. We settled her down in our bed and I took her to the surgery the next morning. The GP said she had flu, prescribed antibiotics and on the Thursday and Friday she took all her various medicines, was sick from time to time, but her temperature kept stable.

Saturday morning was relaxed – I went to town for a hair appointment in the morning and popped into the library to pick up some videos for Hazel to watch. When I got back I thought she looked wrong; she looked grey. So I called the off-duty doctors' surgery. The doctor I spoke to huffed and puffed as he was very busy that day, but said I had better bring her in. We saw a nicer lady doctor who said that Hazel was having trouble breathing and called the hospital to arrange for her admission. I drove her straight there; it was just around the corner. On the way she suddenly said "Mummy, my legs are hurting badly" and had a fearful look in her eyes. It worried me a lot, but I stayed calm for her and felt inside that I just HAD to get her to hospital, as soon as I could. The nurse at Reception carried her to the ward for me. Hazel was heavy; she was at the top of the growth charts for height and weight. She chatted to the nurse on the way about her 4th birthday party, which she was going to have the next Saturday; she was planning to have pass-the-parcel, etc.

The nurse in the children's ward assessed Hazel immediately and she was given a mask to help her breathing. They laid her down on a table and we held hands while a couple of nurses worked around her and tried to find a vein, but she was dehydrated from her flu and they were having difficulty. She fell asleep and while I was pleased for her to have the rest, it worried me and I asked the nurse if it was OK that she fell asleep. She said it was fine, but the thought must have been there that I didn't want her to die even though it hadn't consciously occurred to me that she might.

The consultant arrived and within a couple of minutes Hazel's heart stopped. The crash team was called and so many doctors came to the room that in the end they were turning doctors away because there was not enough space for them. They were trying everything to save her – adrenaline shots, artificial respiration, electric shocks on her chest. It lasted for an hour. I spent almost the whole time talking to her, to try to bring her back. I remember delving into my handbag for chewing gum because my mouth was so dry from talking continuously. In between, the doctors would fire questions at me, "Does she have a rash anywhere?" – "No." "What is her weight?" – "3 stone" and then we would do the mental arithmetic aloud to convert it to kilos for the correct dosage of adrenaline. Sometimes there would be a faint trace of a heartbeat, everyone would go "Sssshh!" and then it would go again. It was so tiring, that hour, that after about 40 minutes I was ready to give up, which I am still ashamed to admit. I had summoned every bit of strength to keep it together, I would not let myself get upset because I had to do everything I could to try and save her. But it was exhausting. And to see her lovely little body subjected to all these medical procedures, it seemed so wrong. I just wanted to protect her.

About 15 minutes after Hazel's heart had stopped, one nurse asked me if there was anyone I would like her to call. I immediately said "No", because I was coping and didn't need anyone's help. Then I realised she meant that my husband should be called because this was serious – so I gave her the telephone number – and then realised that quite possibly Hazel might not come back. Suddenly in all the hustle and bustle my mobile rang and everyone stopped and looked at me. I then had a quick conversation with Mark along the lines of "No everything is not alright, can you get here as soon as possible?" He asked if she had died and I said no.

So then, after an hour the consultant, Mark and I decided that we had to stop; she would have been badly brain damaged even if her heart had started again. They took the tubes and equipment away and we were left on our own with Hazel lying on the table. I cuddled her and couldn't believe how different she felt. "She's not cuddling back" I said to Mark. It felt like she had gone, totally. One of her eyes was open where the doctor had been checking with his light for a response, so I closed it for her. Her toes were so grey. We didn't stay very long with her at all, because it wasn't her anymore. It felt to me like my lovely, alive Hazel had been left in a parallel universe and the world I was on was heading in a different direction and there was nothing I could do.

Everyday life was suddenly so difficult. Mark had some normality still in his life when he returned to work, but my day had a routine which revolved around taking Hazel to nursery. I had to make a new routine. I found it so tiring looking after Shelley because I would have to be normal around her – although I think that was a good thing for me. I would take Shelley out to toddler groups etc. and not talk to anyone. Inevitably in toddler activities mums talk to each other about their children and I hated the awkward negativity that was associated with talking about Hazel. I didn't like seeing the other mums from nursery because I hated that their child was still alive while my little girl had died. In fact I found I didn't have anything in common with anyone any more, except Mark. We were the only two people who understood what each other was going through, and it really brought us closer together. He had similar experiences with male friends – if he brought Hazel up in conversation, there would follow an awkward silence. I didn't like talking to friends and family; often they would say something insensitive, although I did have one great friend who asked if her support was too much or not enough. Most people however had a very shallow perspective on life compared to mine and I did not want to have fun. How could I have fun when the most important person in my whole life had gone forever? Family events were, and still are, the time when Hazel is missing most.

Losing Hazel was impossibly hard but I could cope with it. I reasoned from the start that I could let in all the pain and have the strength to deal with it because my love for Hazel would always be greater than that pain. And I have to believe that I will see her again when I die; I need that hope to keep me going. But the hardest part to cope with was the rest of my life, the outside world that was not all about Hazel and situations and people that could be unpredictably hurtful.

On the night that Hazel died, both Mark and I decided that we wanted more children. I fell pregnant 3 months later, which was tiring but kept us moving forward. Justine was born on 13th November, the day before Hazel's and my birthday. She was a happy, easy baby despite all the crying she heard whilst in my tummy! It is now approaching 4 years since Hazel died and we are expecting baby number 4. Over the last year we have reached a comfortable normality. We think of ourselves as a family of 3 (soon to be 4). We have periods of badly missing Hazel and crying, and she is still as much a part of our family as she ever was - just in a very different way now.

Lucy Guinn

We feel we might be better people for what we have been through, although we wish we hadn't. We both feel we have been plucked out of day to day life; we're not really involved in it any more but we know it is going on. We batten down the hatches quite often at home; people may ring and try to make contact sometimes but we just want us, because you know what you have got then.

Things are starting to matter more to me now the shock element is coming down. I now think about Hazel more which is nice. Songs you hear and that sort of thing affect me more; I used to turn songs off but now I like it - it's a sort of pleasurable pain. As time goes on, although it's meaning more to me, it's meaning less to everyone else except Lucy. To everyone else it's convenient; they can start approaching me again and I will talk normally.

I find it hard especially to talk to other men about Hazel. They're very comfortable when you talk about normal things like sport and pubs and cars, but it's very difficult to talk about Hazel.

I never found it easy to talk but it is quite unavoidable with Lucy because she just does it all the time, talks about Hazel quite emotionally. I have to talk to her; she brings me down, but if I didn't have that release it would be much harder for me. I can go to work and be normal and happy knowing that I will get nicely depressed when I get home because it is unavoidable!

I could never go long without thinking about Hazel. Lucy's job looking after the children is connected to Hazel all the time. When I go to work there isn't a connection. Lucy has encouraged me to put up a picture of Hazel at work, and I'm really glad I have, but I can be doing something and then see the picture and everything flies out the window. I get upset then and think about Hazel - so she has given me a way to get depressed at work too! But that's a good thing.

Mark Guinn

60

Sabah Tanya Hussain

20 April 2000 - 16 April 2007

Story of an Angel

We were a complete and, most importantly, a happy family; myself the mother, my husband Naseem and my lovely children, two girls Sabah and Sabriya and one boy Kaleem. When I was informed that I was pregnant with my first child, Sabah, I was over the moon. I was looking forward to the day that my first child was going to be born. Once Sabah was born it brought me the entire world's happiness and made my feel a complete woman as I now was a mother.

Every day was special; spending my time with my daughter and looking at her grow with time was amazing. Sabah was loved by everyone within the family. She was a happy and cheerful young girl. Sabah was four years old when her sister Sabriya was born; she was so happy as she had someone she could play with. When Sabriya was two years old, I had Kaleem. I then felt that we were a complete family. Sabah would love to play with her brother and sister and, as the eldest, would take responsibility in looking after both young ones.

Sabah was a very responsible and understanding child for her age, always there to cheer you up with the greatest smile and warm hug, which was something that brought me much closer to my eldest daughter. She was more like my best friend who would always be there. While enjoying my everyday life with my family, we would often have family trips to take the kids out.

61

During this period I started to notice that while walking, Sabah would lose balance and would complain that she had a bad headache. This started when she was three and a half years old. One or two months went by and Sabah was still informing me of the same symptoms she was suffering. I decided to take her to the doctors to get her checked out.

A number of months had gone by and I had made several visits with Sabah to the doctor. The only professional advice I received was that it was common for young children to get headaches as they are starting nursery or playgroup. I was also advised to give Calpol when Sabah complained of a headache. At the start I listened to the doctor and acted upon his advice and gave Sabah the medication he advised. A few months went by with no sign of Sabah's headaches getting any better; I started to get worried and decided to take Sabah back to the doctor for him to look into this further.

He seemed very adamant that Sabah was fine and there was nothing wrong with her. I was very worried and stressed about my daughter and her well-being and requested a scan or x-ray to find out why Sabah was getting headaches. The doctor finally referred Sabah to a specialist to examine her further. The specialist advised keeping a diary of all the food Sabah had, which we did. Sabah loved drinking coke, that was one of the things which made her headaches worse.

We were discharged after 6 months with the conclusion that Sabah had migraine, and were told not to give her food that would make her headaches worse. When I requested a scan to be performed I was advised Sabah was too young and the radiation could affect her brain cells, so I left it at that thinking the doctors knew what they were talking about.

Sabah was loved by everyone who knew her. She loved dressing up and applying make up. Every time we were going out she would go into her room and get dressed up; the way she would apply her make up it was as if someone had done it for her! She had so many friends both of her age and older.

Sabah loved going to school. Every day she would wake up before me and would start watching her favourite cartoons. I would take her to school and on the way she would tell me what they planned in school that day. She preferred to come home for lunch as she said the children were too noisy, which would give her headaches. As her school was close to the park, if it was

62

a nice day we would go to the park after school; she loved going on the slide and playing hide and seek with Sabriya.

Sabah still complained of headaches. I took her back to the doctors so many times. The doctor was adamant that she was fine and that nothing was wrong with her even though Sabah herself was complaining about headaches on a consistent basis. We changed surgeries as I thought that could make a difference, but it didn't. I told the new doctor the history of Sabah, and he also said this is common in young children.

Easter holidays came. Sabah said goodbye to all her friends in school and gave her teacher a hug as if she knew she was never coming back. My sister-in-law and her children came to stay in the holidays. Sabah wasn't herself; she would play with them in the garden then she would come back and lay on the sofa. The second week of the Easter holidays, Sabah started vomiting as well as the headaches. I phoned the surgery and was told there was a bug going round, so give her Calpol which I did. But Sabah wasn't getting better, so on the Friday I took her to the doctors. She vomited twice on the way to the surgery. When I was seen by the doctor he didn't even bother checking her; all he said was there is a virus going round, nothing to worry about. I even requested a scan again at that point but he didn't think it was important.

Sabah was getting worse and on Sunday I decided to take her to A&E. After waiting, we were seen by the nurse who wasn't helpful. I told her I had seen my GP on Friday but my daughter's condition was not improving. She checked Sabah's temperature and weight and told us to wait for the doctor to check Sabah. While we were waiting, Sabah wanted to be read a story and my sister read to her. Sabah was seen by the doctor who said they may need to do a scan; he also said as Sabah was dehydrated, they would need to give her glucose. We were taken to a ward after two hours. I asked about Sabah having glucose but the nurse said it had not been prescribed. Another two hours went by and no-one came to see Sabah.

All of a sudden, Sabah vomited and was unconscious. My sister rushed to get the nurse, then the doctors came and said they didn't even know Sabah was in the ward. They then put up a drip; Sabah regained consciousness, the doctors examined her and then went away. After an hour the same thing happened. Sabah was transferred to a private room and on the way regained consciousness. I didn't know what was going on. The doctor said they were going to do a scan. I told the doctor I had been asking for one for the past two years and had been told Sabah was too young to have one because of the radiation. He said 'We can do MRI on babies if we need to'. I couldn't believe what I was hearing, but I was glad that at least Sabah was going to have a scan now.

We took her for her scan; Sabah was talking to the nurses and said she was cold. My husband went in with Sabah while I waited outside with my sister. I could not get the courage to see my daughter in that state. The doctors then sent my husband out of the room and we came back up to the private room. By then my parents and my brothers had come. The doctor called me and my husband to his room. I took my brother with me. The doctor told us my baby had a brain tumour, but they couldn't tell us what kind of tumour it was or how long she had had it. Sabah needed to be transferred to the John Radcliffe Hospital in Oxford that night. I couldn't believe what the doctor was saying; how can my daughter have a brain tumour when in the past I had been told it is migraine which is common in children?

Sabah was taken to Oxford by ambulance and we followed; there was no space in the ambulance because the doctors travelled with her. We got to the hospital at four in the morning; the nurse came to tell us that because Sabah's condition was getting worse they had to do a little operation near her forehead to release pressure straight away. They brought her into the ward; Sabah was covered with needles and so many machines around her, I couldn't believe that was my little girl.

The doctor came to tell us they needed to do another major operation to remove the tumour, but not until they did another scan which he said may be on the Wednesday. All my family was there; we all took turns to go and see Sabah as only two people were allowed at a time. The doctor in charge came to see us and he said they would need to operate as soon as they could. He had seen the images sent by Wycombe Hospital and if they didn't operate straight away, my daughter would not survive. The doctor advised it could take six hours or more to remove the tumour. I said, 'take as long as you want but make my daughter better'. I didn't want to see Sabah in that state; I wanted my daughter to talk to me, play with me, not to lay on a bed with so many needles. We all said our final goodbyes before they took her to start the operation.

All the family went to pray; the only thing we could do was to pray and hope the operation was successful. Every hour seemed so long. I kept asking the nurse how the operation was going but they could not tell us anything. Finally a nurse came to get us. I asked her how the operation was; she said as far as she knew it was ok but couldn't say anything as we needed to speak to the doctor. We waited in the family room, then the doctor came and said, 'I have bad news for you'. He told us Sabah had passed away while they were operating; her heart stopped.

My world turned upside down. My baby, how can that be? I couldn't hear anything else that the doctor was saying; I was so shocked that twenty four hours ago Sabah was in my arms and now she is so far away.

They gave us a room where we all stayed with Sabah. As I sat next to Sabah's bed, I couldn't believe my daughter would never be able to speak to me; she was just laying there. It was the worst nightmare. I kept on imagining Sabah opening her eyes or getting up and saying, 'Mummy why are you crying? I am here', but unfortunately none of that happened. The doctor then said they may have to do a post mortem, which we refused. My daughter had suffered so much on her own; I was not going to let them cut her into pieces.

In Islam we have to have the funeral as soon as we can. My parents arranged everything. Sabah's funeral was on Tuesday at the mosque where she used to go to read Arabic. So many people came to her funeral; all her teachers from her school, her mosque teachers and all her friends' parents. Sabah's funeral was like it was someone well known, someone who's been around for a while. She was only six years old. Everyone who spoke to me on that day said they couldn't believe this had happened to Sabah. They all said how wonderful she was and how much they loved her.

Sabah died four days before her seventh birthday. She had so many plans for her birthday. She said she was going to have a big party with a bouncy castle, which we had arranged. Instead, all of us were there but Sabah was so far away. We had a memorial for her on her birthday.

When we got Sabah's pathology report it was estimated that Sabah had had a brain tumour for two years. The tumour was an astrocytoma; when I looked on the internet all the symptoms -headaches, vomiting, clumsiness - were what my daughter had. How had the doctors missed all this?

My angel has gone to a better world where there's no suffering. She was so brave and patient; the headaches she was getting were not normal headaches but Sabah kept strong. People go to see doctors because they feel ill and need help and advice from professionals. I knew Sabah was not well at all, but the professionals were stating she was fine. Can they explain how she was fine? No they can't, because it's too late. If I had known Sabah was suffering from a brain tumour and the doctors had done what they were supposed to, it could have been different. She would still be here today if she was treated earlier.

It's been over six months since I have lost my angel. I can't express how difficult it's been without Sabah. Every day I think about Sabah, how it would be if she was still here, the things we would do together. Sabah is missed by everyone who knew her; Sabriya her little sister always talks about her and asks me why did Sabah leave us and go. I do try and explain to her. We are lost without Sabah; she was an angel sent from above, and had to leave us. I go to her grave, pray and talk to her. We take roses to lay on her grave because she loved roses.

We all have to carry on living our lives; the only thing that is keeping me going is my two children. I have to be strong for them; if it wasn't for them God knows what would have happened.

I hope and pray no mother goes through what I have been through.

Sofia Bi Hussain

66

Lewie Steven Charlie Jones

7 January 2004 - 31 July 2005

Lewie

I had an amniocentesis at 23 weeks and found out I was having a boy! What do you do with a boy? I had two beautiful girls, Charlie aged 11 and Imogen aged 4, who had both been a dream. Didn't boys roll around in mud and pick their noses? But Lewie was born on the 7th January 2004, weighing a healthy 8lbs, and he was absolutely adorable. We all fell in love with him instantly.

He was such a character and a flirt! From 6 months old, if complete strangers dared to ignore him whilst out shopping he would shout at them until they noticed him. Then he would give them a beaming cheeky smile and they were hooked! Lewie was brown eyed, blonde haired and by the age of 18 months had a lovely tan. We used to call him our "surfer dude". In the July of 2005 when Lewie was 18 months old, he came down with a chesty cough - nothing to worry about - and was prescribed his first lot of antibiotics and was on the road to recovery. Two weeks after the initial diagnosis I noticed he was still quite sleepy and lethargic. Everyone said this was normal as the weather was so hot, but I wasn't convinced having had two other children. I decided to make an appointment for the following Wednesday to see our doctor - I thought perhaps Lewie was anaemic - but we never made that appointment.

On the Saturday morning we all got up as usual. Lewie was in a brilliant mood and ate all his breakfast and mine! Later on, my husband and I went food shopping and took Lewie with us. Again he was shouting at everyone and showing off, and in the car coming home he was dancing to the music on the

67

radio. We looked at each other and said, "Isn't it nice to have the old Lewie back".

At home I was busy cooking tea. Lewie was moaning so I asked Charlie to put him in his high chair. He gave out a piercing cry and I knew something was wrong; I thought he had trapped his fingers or something. I went running into the dining room and at once knew it was very serious. Lewie was completely blue around the mouth, retching, very grey and clammy with sweat. I grabbed him and ripped his clothes off and shouted at my husband to call an ambulance. He said there wasn't time, so we all piled into the car.

When we arrived at the hospital, they rushed us through and put Lewie on oxygen. He then seemed to perk up and they said there was nothing wrong with him; they had x-rayed him and done other tests but all seemed fine. It was now getting late and they decided to keep us in overnight. Lewie was pretty restless and in the morning we had toast and juice together – a very special meal – and Lewie was x-rayed again, but there was nothing to report. A paediatrician checked Lewie over and gave him the all clear. I still wasn't convinced about his breathing, so they agreed we could stay another night for observation. Two hours later my beautiful baby boy was dead.

Lewie's oxygen levels had dropped and I had taken him to a nurse. They tried to get a line into his little hands, but he arrested. They spent over an hour trying to get him back. It was all a blur at the time but I know my husband and twin sister were there with us. My sister then had to go and get our daughters and bring them back to the hospital. How she ever made that journey, I will never know. We then had to tell our beautiful daughters, who had never done anything mean or horrible in their lives, that their little brother was dead.

Our darling Lewie had to have a post mortem and actually died of a condition called hypertrophic cardiomyopathy – a thickening of the muscles of the heart. This condition shows no signs. You sometimes read of teenagers dropping down dead whilst playing football – well this was that condition, but it is extremely rare in someone as young as Lewie.

The girls decorated Lewie's coffin with pictures of his favourite things: Winnie the Pooh, Thomas the Tank, dogs and all our hand prints. We wanted the girls to be so involved and not left out. This has really helped, especially for Imogen who was only six at the time. At Lewie's funeral the girls each chose a piece of music, Immi chose "The Crazy Frog" as Lewie loved this song and it meant we all walked out of the service with a smile on our faces. I stood up and read a poem. I didn't know if I could, but I wanted so much to do something for Lewie as I would never be able to make a speech at his 18th, or sing happy birthday to him, so those thoughts gave me the strength to go ahead.

Charlie, our eldest daughter, has been so loving and caring, always worrying if we are upset, checking if I have had a good day and seeing if her dad is OK. He worshipped his little boy – "My boy" he would call him. She has her bad times – "Lewie moments" we call them, and I hope I am always around or aware when they both need me. I didn't want to be so wrapped up in my own grief that I ignored the girls and hopefully with the help of CBC I have done OK.

I went through, and still do go through, very strange emotions. I feel very strongly about my grief for Lewie and almost feel possessive over it. I feel only I, my husband and our girls have the right to it. Everyone else can grieve for Lewie, but I don't want to hear about it. He was our boy and we lost him, they didn't. But of course they did and I know I am being irrational, but it is all I have left of him. So if we send a balloon up, I want us to be the first to do it. I wanted first choice of flowers for his funeral. I wanted to spend time with just my immediate family on his birthdays. I don't want to watch other people cry for him. When my eldest daughter read a speech she had written for a conference for CBC, I didn't want any other family members there apart from my twin sister, because I wanted to build more memories that are exclusive to us. As time passes these feelings ease and I am not so possessive, but it still takes hold every now and again.

We talk of Lewie constantly and do many things to celebrate his amazing but short life. Our lives have been changed forever. It will never be the same again but we still have a lot of living to do. It has made us all grow up and in turn we all appreciate life and what it has to offer in a much simpler version – we don't take anything for granted.

We are very fortunate that we have been able to go on and have another child – a little boy called Ben. He has been our medicine and we are very honoured that we have been blessed with another child.

Lewie has become our shining star, our white fluffy feather on the ground, a dog with a cheeky face, a light breeze across our face. He is everywhere and we all carry him safely locked in our hearts.

Toni Jones

69

My first memory of Lewie is at the hospital the day after he was born. He was really small, swamped by a mountain of blanket. To be honest I didn't even see him at first as I was looking in the little cot, not expecting him to be on the big bed. I couldn't believe that I had waited all this time and yet when mum said "Charlie do you want to hold him?" I almost said no. He looked too small and fragile to hold and my hands suddenly felt like big planks of wood. I was very annoyed when Imogen (my four year old sister) held him with complete confidence and looked as though she had been doing it for years. I didn't want to hold him but I didn't want anyone else to either. When other visitors turned up I was worried that one of them would drop him, but they didn't.

And as soon as I could I began to bath and change him, feed him, put him to bed, take him on walks and push him in the swing. I used to lift him onto Imogen's lap so she could take him down the slide. Together Imogen and I entertained and spoiled him as if he was a king – King Lewie! I remember hiding behind the door watching him and Imogen playing, both of them giggling. Then Lewie would notice me and climb down backwards off the sofa and toddle over for a hug.

'Lewie-blue-shoes' he became because of the colour of his shoes. And on birthdays (with the help of mum) we would receive a birthday card from him with a blue foot print. Dad would take him with him to his workshop, where he would sit at Dad's desk and eat jaffa cakes. He would toddle round with a spanner in one hand and a soggy biscuit in the other. "He is just like you" people would say to Dad who couldn't help but smile. "Where's ma boy?" Dad would say as he came in from work and out Lewie would run into Dads arms shrieking "My Daddy", but soon he would be off playing in the garden with his "ca-cars".

On Saturday 30th of July 2005 Mum decided we needed to go out. "Charlie can you get Lewie in the car?" Imogen moaned "I want to" but I replied "Imo you can't reach". As I got Lewie in the car a feather flew down and landed on his nose. I tickled him and told him to blow, but he didn't understand and licked it instead. I laughed and just brushed it away. When we returned home from shopping and I got Lewie out of his car seat the same feather was caught on his T-shirt. I said "Oh look Lewie it's back".

That evening Lewie was really moaney and restless. Mum was cooking so I put him in his highchair but he screamed out and started retching! Mum grabbed

70

him and stripped him down to his vest, he was really sweating. " Is it a fish bone?" Dad asked. " I don't know!" Mum shouted "Just call an ambulance". "There's no time, we'll drive ourselves". Mum held Lewie, who kept retching and his eyes started rolling in his head. It was very scary but also very exciting. We got to the hospital and the lady rushed us straight through. They wired him up to a machine to check his oxygen. They needed him to eat to see if anything was stuck in his throat but he wouldn't, he just wanted to sleep.

Imo and I were starving so Dad took us home. At about half past nine Mum called Dad to say she had to stay the night and could he bring some spare clothes. Imo wanted to go with Dad but I said I would be all right at home. You have no idea how much I regret not going back, to see him one last time. I just stayed at home and watched television – a typical teenager, too lazy to get up. I will never forget that.

The next day some family started to arrive for a BBQ. Dad explained that Lewie and Mum were in hospital but should be home soon. At about twelve o'clock Dad was told to come to the hospital. I said I was coming too but Grandma told me not to, which made me really angry. At 2 o'clock Auntie Lisa came and told Imogen and me to come with her to the hospital.

She had been crying. I kept thinking "I know Lewie is poorly but you don't need to cry – he is coming home soon". Then I thought maybe he has died but I told myself off for being so stupid. We arrived at the hospital and Imogen noticed Thomas the Tank Engine stickers on the wall. "I'm glad Lewie is in this bit, he will like these." Lisa didn't answer. Then I felt crushed. I didn't want to go any further. I knew it – I could feel he had died. Just by looking at my Auntie's face I could tell. Imogen's little voice seemed distant and it didn't feel like me walking, I looked at Imogen and I knew what was about to happen and I felt so guilty, like it was my fault, she still had no idea what was about to happen. We got to some big double doors and walked straight through, but a nurse stopped me. "I'll bring your Mum and Dad out." "No!" I screamed and I felt myself push past her. I hated her. I felt like saying how dare you. I completely forgot about Imogen though I knew she was still holding my hand.

Mum and Dad came to the door, I knew Mum had been crying, but I had never seen my Dad cry before – it was a shock. I looked into my Dad's eyes and he looked away. "What?" but nobody answered. "What's happened, what's wrong?" I shouted. "He's gone" Mum said. "Your joking!" I screamed "Stop it now your joking – no!" Looking back I feel terrible. I was completely selfish. I left Imogen and shrugged off the nurses that tried to comfort me. "Do you want to hold him?" Mum asked. I snatched his body out of her arms and stupidly thought it would be like a fairy tale and if my tears fell on his cheek he would wake up. I sang Barney and Thomas the Tank Engine and the Wiggles over and over in my head hoping he would hear and wake up.

We spent ages there. Auntie Lisa took Imo home. My Nanny and Grampy came to the hospital and the police – CID. I wasn't allowed to listen when they interviewed my Mum and Dad which made me so angry. "My Boy" Dad whispered "He's just asleep." Finally we had to leave. Saying goodbye was the hardest thing that I have ever had to do. We left Lewie with 'Dog-Dog' his favourite soft toy. We got in the car. I sat next to his empty car seat, his juice bottle and coat, and as I got out of the car I noticed something white on the floor. It was the feather – our feather. I still have it, I always will!

For days afterwards the house was full of friends, family, coroners, doctors and health visitors and so many cards and flowers. The phone didn't stop! At first I was excited to see everyone and I rushed to answer the door, but soon it really hit me why they were here and I was sick of hearing Mum tell the same story and I just wanted them to all go away. Dad stayed upstairs – he couldn't face seeing everyone. At his funeral there were so many people some had to stand at the back. There were his nursery helpers, people from where my Mum and Dad work and people from my school who I hardly ever speak to. It was lovely.

Imogen has said, of that time:

> *"I can remember Lewie being sad and not happy but I could make him laugh. On the way to the hospital with Mummy and Daddy I was sad because I thought something was going to happen. When I was with Auntie Lisa I was kind of happy but I didn't really know what was going on. When I found out Lewie had died I was very sad because he was my only brother. I wanted to go home but I don't really know why."*

In the first few days after Lewie died Imogen kept asking my mum to take her temperature. "Why?" Mum asked. "Because I want to be dead like Lewie, then I can be with him". Imogen has asked "Why did Lewie have to die?" and "Can we go and see his grave?" even before we had had his funeral. After

Lewie had gone to the John Radcliffe Hospital for a post mortem she asked me "When they took Lewie to the other hospital did they put him in a car seat?" Lewie had already passed away and I knew that he would have travelled differently but to a 6 year old it is a completely different story.

It was clear she had heard people talking but only understood half of it. Lewie had Dog-Dog and other special toys with him in his coffin but after the funeral Imogen asked if she could have Dog-Dog. "Has he been burnt?" she kept asking and no one knew what to say. In another example Imogen said to my Auntie "When we see Lewie in heaven will he be the same or will we not be able to play with him because he is all stiff and dead like this?" (and she went all stiff). I love the way she is so frank and just comes out with things that most adults would dare not say.

Even though Lewie died young he did so much in his little life. He went to Disneyland Paris, where he was stung by a wasp, Italy where he spent nearly all day in the swimming pool, Switzerland where he climbed a mountain, France where he and Imogen sailed practically the whole of the Dordogne river in a little dingy and Devon where he became number one surf dude!

Grief affects us all in different ways. For me, I now feel that there is absolutely no point to school! Why should I sit in lessons that I hate, with people that have no idea how I feel, people who's biggest problem is what to wear to the party on Friday, not 'I wonder if Mum will be all right tonight' or 'I can't bear to see my Dad cry'. Why should I sit at school listening to a teacher shouting at me for not paying attention. It would not even come into her head that I could be thinking of Lewie, because what does he mean to her? Nothing, She doesn't even know he existed. I can't bring myself to tell people the truth and sometimes I just want to scream as yet another of my friends comes to me with their problems, but selfishly to me they are not problems anymore, not compared to what my family have been through.

Some days I'm fine but on other days I hope that when I close my eyes and go to sleep I won't wake up. I hate the way that I will be watching television and then a little boy will come on screen and my whole body tenses. I wait and I pray that my mum isn't crying. I can't bear to look, I can't bear it any more. I hate the way I put on this front – if I feel sad at school I just tell my friends I left something in a different room and I pretend to go and get it when really I go to the toilets to try and calm myself down. Only one of my friends

73

has noticed my feelings - in a poem she wrote about me in an English lesson she said:

> "She hides her feelings behind words on a page, drama and her art work."

I didn't know what to say to her, but she just looked at me and smiled .

I find myself not saying things to my family because it might make them sad. It is awful watching a man cry but in a way it is worse watching him tying to hide it. Sometimes all you need is a hug but other times it's nice to be left alone.

Death is not an embarrassing thing. Do not be afraid to mention someone's lost one. It is not possible for you to upset them any more than they already are. If they do not want to talk then they will tell you. I have found that at school people who once talked to me now avoid me. People need to learn to ask questions - I love talking about Lewie. Again everyone is different.

Involve children - do not hide the truth. Together my family and I decorated Lewie's coffin with pictures of his favourite things like dogs and Winnie-the-Pooh. If you have children and you don't know how to explain to them, there are so many books such as 'The Lonely Tree' which my sister has found helpful. The film 'Finding Neverland' is wonderful. as it shows adults' and children's perceptions of death and helps you remember happy memories of before that time, so that you are not crushed by your grief.

Lewie died at 19 months old of Hypertrophic Cardiomyopathy, an undiagnosed heart condition that shows no symptoms - our lives have been changed forever.

Charlie, Lewie's sister

74

Poem read at Lewie's funeral:

FAIRY CASTLE

*In a fairy castle
just beyond my eyes,
my baby plays with angels toys
that money cannot buy.*

*Who am I to bring him back
into this world of strife?
No, play on my baby,
you have eternal life.*

*At night when all is silent
yet sleep forsakes my eyes,
I hear his tiny footsteps
come running to my side.*

*His tiny hands caress me
so tenderly and sweet.
I breathe a sigh and say a prayer,
embrace him in my sleep.*

*No, I have a treasure
that I hold above all other,
I have known true glory
for I am still his mother.*

Angus Lawson

12 October 2004 –
7 September 2006

Angus

Angus died just over a year ago. Out of my sight for minutes, unaware of the danger, he drowned in someone's swimming pool. He was 23 months old. I fought hard to save his life, believing every minute he would take a breath, open his eyes and the nightmare would be over.

I looked at the expressions of the ambulance men, the doctors, the nurses; I watched as the fervour of their actions slowed and I knew hope was fading. In the end it became clear there was no hope and I didn't want them to put him through any more. I took him in my arms, found a room and our day ended as it had started together, cuddling.

In the days following Angus' death I spent all my time either with Angus reading him his favourite stories or planning his funeral. We had a small family-only funeral and two days later a memorial service to which we invited anyone who wanted to attend. Hundreds came. I had a very clear idea of how I wanted the services to be and Angus was at the centre of everything I did. Looking back I have no idea how I managed to function. I think in a way the demands of the funeral gave me the opportunity to mother Angus just a little longer.

The support we received from family, friends and even people we hardly knew was and is truly humbling. Nick and I drew a lot of strength from the kindness we were shown. We were given a perspective of humanity we did not know existed. In this respect, we were exceptionally lucky and had we not felt all that love and compassion I think we could have given up on life.

Hope was also possible as I was pregnant with Angus' brother Mungo. Together we shared a few weeks as a blissfully happy family; happy with Angus, happy to be having a baby. I remember when I told Nick and Angus about being pregnant. We were in the kitchen, Angus sitting on Nick's knee, Angus not really understanding but smiling nonetheless. Throughout the pregnancy I lived with a conflicting mixture of emotions. I was terrified I would lose the baby but at the same time I was reluctant to acknowledge I was going to have another little boy. I could not imagine being able to love like that again. Before Angus died I had not worried about loving another child in the same way I loved him. I believed that love was infinite. Without Angus it was hard to have any conviction about anything.

When I lost Angus I lost the heart of my life. I had woken up every morning to the sound of "Mummy", the rhythm of my day was set by Angus, we were never apart. He showed me joy I had never imagined. I was truly blessed and I knew it. Then nothing. Silence. Pain. Emptiness. Unimaginable loneliness. Time becomes your enemy. The days pass so slowly, every second taking me further from Angus. To find a way of surviving in this new world and to feel close to Angus I walk and I work in the garden. In the early days and weeks, when I couldn't bear to stay in bed any longer lying with the silence, I was able to feel some calm walking in the mornings filling my mind with Angus. When Nick went back to work I could break up the day and live with the loneliness walking. I find walking gives me glimpses of nature's majesty, windows to a world beyond me where Angus now belongs.

I feel closest to Angus in the garden. The day he died, Angus and I had been together in the garden pottering about, I had given him his own pair of gloves, we had laughed. Angus' birthday came shortly after he died. I knew I wanted to spend the day planting, creating my own piece of nature in his image. There is a wooded area in our garden where Angus used to play and where one of his magic dinosaur trees lives. My hope is, in time, to grow a vision of blue planting bluebells, scilla and muscari as a vivid reminder of his incredible eyes. Working in the garden I feel engaged in life and my imagination is occupied away from the flashbacks that pierce my mind. I am very aware of the butterflies and the birds and in some way I connect them with Angus' spirit. The robins follow me about the garden and are special companions. It is a story about a robin that drew me to Angus' brother's name, Mungo. This bond between Angus and Mungo gives me some comfort. Mungo will only know his brother in death; I find this heartbreaking but Angus will always be part of Mungo's life.

When Angus died I cried over and over again "I can't bear it". Having to live a life when your child has died is unbearable. Over a year on and the pain is unchanged. There are so many hopes to let go of and very few dreams to hold on to. Every day is a marathon, some more arduous than others, and exhaustion becomes a normal way of life. Part of my soul died with Angus and I am a different person. I don't know that person and my loved ones don't know that person. This is an upsetting, lengthy adjustment for everyone. I think grief is a lonely journey and no two are the same. No one can make your journey for you. No one can tell you how to travel and no one knows where you will end up. Much of the writing around grief talks about acceptance being the final "stage". I have no idea what this means. I know the day I die I will still wake up wanting to spend it with Angus. I know I will never make any sense of why Angus died. I know this means part of me will be tormented forever.

I draw my hope from the love I can still feel. I have a wonderful family and some exceptional friends who show me uncompromising support and constant understanding. I have Nick. Our ways of grieving are very different. For Nick, the charity he set up in Angus' memory helps him manage his grief and for me it is the garden. Much of Nick's day-to-day life is public and most of mine is private. Often we go in opposing directions but we are still able to meet and love each other. I have Mungo and he has brought me back to life in a way. Before Mungo was born I was very afraid my sadness for Angus would prevent me from loving him. I was almost more afraid that if I chose to love Mungo I would in some way be leaving Angus. Mungo was born and the love I felt was so strong and entirely instinctive. I have not had to choose between my two boys. I love them both completely. My heart holds their love and my sadness and the two do not compete.

Life carries on. I was made aware of this just minutes after Angus died. As I lay holding him, I heard laughter outside. The difference between our worlds was painfully clear. As time passes, functioning in daily life gets steadily easier although some things remain impossible. The sense of being different, separated from other people's normality endures. Mungo has pulled me away from a lot of the seclusion I had chosen for myself. I can laugh, sing and even dance for him – all things I imagined would be too difficult. He wholly engages me and I can mother him without compromise. There are times when I feel too distant from Angus and that is when I head out to the garden. I know I have a future with Mungo and I know I can look forward to celebrating everything his life becomes. I live with the constant fear he will die too.

Angus came into my life and opened my soul to indescribable love. We shared a world together that can never be recreated. I miss his gentleness and the magic he showed me how to find in everyday life. I am so sad that he did not get the chance to live the wonderful life that would have been rightfully his. I wish I had had the chance to meet the person he would have become. My hope is that one day I may be so lucky. Till then I carry his love in my heart. At least I never have to say goodbye.

Kara Lawson

On 7th September 2006 my son Angus drowned in a tragic accident that was such a freak outlier of an event we still struggle with the statistical mercilessness of its improbability. It would have been his second birthday a month later. He was everything to me and until his death, our family life was complete.

Regardless of fortune's cruelty the hardest part of coping with the death of someone you cherish is that you become almost instantly far from love and feel that it will be absent forever from your life. After Angus died I remember reading the words of St. John of the Cross talk of the "dark night of the soul," such an apt description of the terrible inner journey which throws everything you have known and believed into question.

One thing though that has been revelatory has been the good I have seen in people. Impossible to detail have been the qualities of people who have helped us. I decided very soon after Angus died that I wanted to create something permanent in his name. I have a very simple mathematical ideal of offsetting a negative with a positive. If our son was to die, then only good would come from this event. Within a week of his death I started setting up

79

a Memorial Trust in his name – the Angus Lawson Memorial Trust (ALMT - www.almt.org). I realise now that in the immediate aftermath, I drove ahead and distracted myself with this to the exclusion of all else and distanced myself from the people I loved. In hindsight, I realise I deliberately created a vehicle to mask my grief.

Six months after he died I really suffered. The ALMT had grown and allowed me to keep mentioning his name in a number of different contexts. All the projects we funded around the world were eponymously titled and I could speak his name in relation to the Trust without people recoiling. There did, though, become a point when I had to stop keeping him alive and grieve for his parting. It is a subtle balance between physically letting go and sustaining the memory of him.

I began to have counselling and was prescribed anti-depressants. I started to work on my relationships with those closest to me and began to adjust to the dreadful reality that my son was dead.

I am still very involved in the Trust but it is not now to the exclusion of all else. My son's Trust is now more than the knee-jerk reaction to our grief, and is the expression of people's goodness to which I alluded earlier. The phrase I used back in December of last year for the website has become so strikingly pertinent to describe the evolution of the ALMT: "No man or woman stands so straight as when they stoop to help a child."

The ALMT is already making huge inroads into children's lives. The Trust is purely for needy children with the idea that Angus is lighting their lives as the angel he now is. After the death of a child you become so accustomed to sadness that it becomes a bedfellow that never leaves you. Nevertheless, over time appear chinks of light; the joy of Angus's brother Mungo growing up, the moment when my wife and I unconsciously laugh about something without being thrown back into despair afterwards; the compassion shown from the strangest quarters that can brighten up a day.

Something changes forever when your child dies and there are many phases of grief. I have alienated a lot of people, but I am learning and I am still unflinching in my determination to make what is my darkness also my light.

Nick Lawson

80

Zoe Le

5th April 2005 –
28th October 2007

Zoe

Forever love, you'll always be in our hearts

God gives life, and God takes life away, and the taking away is so terribly painful because what he has given us is so special.

The 5th April 2005 Zoe our precious youngest baby was born. Her little life has never been easy with her unexplained ill health. She started her endless tests when she was just over 20 days old. Zoe couldn't manage to put on weight, her condition was identified as very rare metabolic disease, despite numerous tests there wasn't any specified diagnosis. Zoe's condition still remains a mystery now and forever.

With her undiagnosed condition and frequent hospital visits we couldn't see the future; we were worried, constantly feeling helpless and miserable. However Zoe never gave up. She was determined, tough and strong. She always managed to smile. She fought until the last minutes of her life.

Zoe has an older sister named Grace with an age gap of 18 months. It was a tremendous joy and happiness to witness both of them grow together. Grace and Zoe loved each other intensely. Grace is gentle by nature, but Zoe is strong minded – she knows what she wants. I remember one day coming home from work and cuddling both of them. I sat Zoe on my right lap and

Grace on the left lap. They both wanted me to read them a story. Grace wanted me to read "Sleeping Beauty" but Zoe wanted me to read "The Very Hungry Caterpillar" instead. Zoe grabbed Grace's book and threw it away so that Daddy can read her book instead.

Zoe has been our boss for 2½ years and now she has gone. We suddenly lost our minds; we're at a loss and don't know what to do. Without her in our daily life we lose part of our body, life is not complete without her. We miss that smiley face. We miss that loud voice and the non-stop chatting. We miss that demanding and lively Zoe. Because of Zoe's condition she required constant care with her NG feeds and oxygen; the loving bond Zoe has developed with the rest of the family is more intense than compared to a normal child.

The death of Zoe is very traumatic because it was unexpected. She was so strong and we made a decision for her to have a Gastrostomy, Nissen Fundoplication and Portacath to improve her quality of life. The operation itself took 8 hours to complete. It was the longest wait of my life! She was fine after the operation and we thought Zoe will come home in about 3 to 4 days after that. But then she developed acute kidney failure and taking on body fluid. Zoe eventually went into PICU and was on the kidney filtration machine whilst she was under anaesthetic to filter out the toxic fluid in the blood. She was in PICU for more than 2 weeks and was under sedation and on the ventilation machine all that time. We were there by her bedside and were helpless. We watched our Zoe's life slowly drifting away from us. She developed so many complications including Disseminated Intravascular Coagulation (DIC), blood clotting and finally we were told she had brain damage too. Her body just couldn't take it any more. The Doctors finally did the test to confirm whether Zoe's brain had died. We were given the last moment to be with Zoe and hold her in our arms when the ventilation machine was finally switched off. She died on 28th October 2007.

Up to now it seems so surreal I still cannot believe this is happening - the thought of never again being able to hold Zoe and hear her say "Pa" again can be most difficult to bear. It seems even more unfair that death has taken away Grace's best friend whom she loved dearly. The loss of Zoe has left a permanent gap in Grace's life. With Zoe's death sometimes I am at a loss as to what to say or do to help Grace cope with what has happened. I've noticed the effect it has had on Grace - she seems to be more insecure and worries that her mummy and daddy might disappear and never come back again like Zoe.

Zoe is a special girl. We've agreed that she is an angel sent by God to us and only for a little while. In her short little life she brought us tremendous joy and happiness regardless of her bothering ill health. She was such a cheerful girl she smiled and made friends with anyone on the buses, in the shops, at the hospital - anywhere. We are going to pay her our endless remembrance and missing. We know that it is a huge loss to us to lose Zoe but we understand that Zoe has a new mission from God, she's going to spray happiness to other families - she's the happy angel from heaven. We're grateful for having her for 2½ years. Zoe's taught us to appreciate our lives, to appreciate love and treasure what we've got.

As part of my healing process I am creating a web site (www.foreverlove.org.uk) to share our experiences of the deep pain that we feel when we lost Zoe. This is my project and it is my way of coming to terms with my loss.

Diep and Peiling Le

Too Soon

This was a life that had hardly begun
No time to find your place in the sun
No time to do all you could have done
But we loved you enough for a lifetime

No time to enjoy the world and its wealth
No time to take life down from the shelf
No time to sing the song of yourself
Though you had enough love for a lifetime

Those who live long endure sadness and tears
But you'll never suffer the sorrowing years
No betrayal, no anger, no hatred, no fears
Just love - only love - in your lifetime.

Author unknown

Liam Francis Logue

1 June 1987 – 26 June 2005

Liam

Liam was a typical 18-year-old boy. He wasn't sporty but he would give anything a go. From the time he was a toddler, he was always interested in how things were put together. He would always want to help his dad or granddad with DIY and tinkering about with cars. On many occasions his granddad found screws and things poked into his car locks! He was inquisitive and wanted to know how things worked.

He was very sociable, had lots of friends, and was very popular because he was great fun. He was a tease and teased everybody. In his social side he took after his dad – I am a bit of a home bird. But we always enjoyed each other's company. He was just really silly. I can be silly and together we were really silly! I was never embarrassing to him. What was lovely about him was that he was never afraid to be loving in public. He would always give me a hug and kiss no matter who was around.

As he grew he got into cars in a big way. He loved them. He was in the final week of a diploma course at the Langley Campus of East Berkshire College and had a place lined up at Oxford Brookes University. He was just loving it, loving life basically. He was working on restoring a mini and he wanted to do well and be rich. For his 18th birthday, he wasn't interested in designer clothes; he was more interested in quality craftsmanship and wanted a particular pen. "When I am rich," he said, "I'm going to sign all of my cheques with this pen."

The day he died was just an ordinary Sunday. Liam had a part time job at Halfords and got in at about five o'clock in the afternoon. Although Rob and

I were, and still are, separated, we spend a lot of time together. Rob had been here at home and had cooked Liam's favourite – roast dinner. Because of the family's other commitments, it had been weeks since we had all sat down and eaten together. Liam walked through the door after work and said, "Wicked, roast dinner – my favourite!"

After dinner Liam went to Hughenden Park, a big open park, to meet his girlfriend Bryony and play rounders. The park was mid-way between their two houses and they both drove down. They then had a nice innocent summer evening together.

At around 10.30 Bryony pulled out of the car park and went one way home, and Liam pulled out to go the other way.

In less than a minute he had his accident, on the main stretch of road. His car ended up on the wrong side of the road and he had a head-on collision with a car coming the other way. There were no witnesses to say why. He came round a bend, just an inexperienced driver, and didn't approach the bend properly. He wasn't speeding, he wasn't on his mobile phone, and he hadn't been drinking. There was no obvious reason for it.

Two cars came along behind the car that he hit. The drivers got out and phoned an ambulance and realised that something was very wrong with Liam. They got him out of the car and tried to do mouth-to-mouth on him. They really tried to save him, but it was almost instant really. At the inquest they said that he was moaning a little so he must have been alive for a bit. I don't know exactly what his injuries were because I didn't really want to know. It doesn't change anything.

I had been out for the evening and got home at around 11.45pm. Rob was still there with Amy and our twins, Christopher and Daniel. Amy is a mother hen and worries a lot about everybody, which she gets from me, but I try and control my fears whereas she worries all the time. She kept saying, "Liam only went to Hughenden Park to play rounders, why isn't he home yet?" But he was so wrapped up in Bryony that I really wasn't worried. I said, "He is having a nice time with Bryony," thinking they were probably having a kiss and a cuddle in the car park. Amy decided to ring Liam but thought he would be annoyed, so she rang his number and threw the phone at me to talk to him. But of course he didn't answer his phone. I said,"Don't worry, he will be home soon." I had no sense of foreboding at all.

At 12.30am I had literally just gone to bed and Rob had just gone home when there was a knock at the door, which I presumed must be Liam. My immediate thought was that he must have forgotten his keys. Then I realised that he couldn't have as he was driving, using his keys. I then thought that for some reason he didn't have the front door key on his ring. When I opened the door there was a policeman standing outside. He asked if this was where Liam lived. I said yes. He then asked if I was Liam's mum. I said yes. He then asked if there was anyone in house with me and I then knew something awful had happened.

He just said, "You have lost him".

I ran away screaming, ran into the sitting room crying and screaming. The policeman stayed in the hall. Amy came downstairs and was fantastic. She was hysterical as well but took over and phoned Rob, crying and screaming over the phone. He only lives 500 yards away and came straight back round.

Amy rang me to say "Dad, Dad come home, Liam's dead." That still makes me go cold when I remember the phone call. In a split second our life changed. **Rob**

The Police Family Liaison Officer was fantastic. He gave us space, was there but in the background. He waited outside until we had calmed down a little bit and then came in to talk to us and very gently went through the series of events that had happened. He was very kind and gave us as much detail as we needed to know but not so much that it was awful. At the inquest I couldn't listen to what had happened or look at pictures of Liam's car.

He said, very importantly, that Liam still looked like Liam. It meant a lot that he said that. He explained that he had been taken to Wycombe Hospital and they would contact us to come and see him. By this time it was one o'clock. He said they would contact us in the morning to see him and I just said "I need to go now". I just wanted to be with him and wanted us all to be together. I didn't want Liam to be by himself. In fact I took him a photograph of all of us so that he didn't feel that he was alone.

When we initially saw him in the hospital he was in a side room in A&E and just looked like he was asleep - he had no scars or anything. He used to muck about and pretend he was asleep and you would go up and give him a kiss, and I almost imagined that he was going to do that again. With hindsight, it was probably best to see him straight away.

The staff at the hospital were amazing – it was obviously very difficult for them. I remember in particular one really young nurse, possibly a student who just came and sat with him and cried. It meant a lot.

When we got back from the hospital it was about 5am. Rob said, "I need to phone people and tell them what has happened." I couldn't understand how he could consider doing that; if you tell people then it makes it real. From 7am he started ringing round. He needed to do it, but I couldn't bear to make those phone calls. He was in 'trying to sort everything out' mode. He needed to know that we would get support from other people, which we did.

Initially, because it was such a shock, the thought of contacting a funeral director or planning the service was a million miles away. Fortunately a friend of ours works for a funeral director and she very kindly came to see us to explain what would happen next. She wanted us to know the things we should be thinking about and considering, and it seemed appropriate that we used the people she worked for. Liam was in the hospital for a couple of days before they then went to collect him.

We went to see Liam at the funeral directors. Amy was adamant she didn't want to see him in a coffin so he was always on a bed. It gave us the opportunity to be with him and talk to him. We went to see him a lot – it really did help. I lost my dad when I was 12; one minute he was at home then he died in the night, was taken away and I never saw him again. I used to dream about my dad quite a lot – that he had been away for a long time and came back. It was great, but then I would wake up and he wasn't there which was really hard. From a personal point of view I felt if I were to see Liam it would help me accept what had happened. I have never had a dream like that about Liam. I think in my head that going to see him has helped me to accept that he has died.

It was almost two weeks after the accident that we had Liam's funeral – quite a long time but we wanted to make sure we got it right and had time to think about what we needed to think about. I always felt that it was very important that everyone was included in the decision-making. From our first discussions, Amy was determined she was going to speak. We all felt we would like a role to play. She and the boys had an input into the order of service and took it to the printers. Our local vicar who helped plan the service was concerned for everybody. He kept saying to Amy, "On the day you may find it very difficult to stand up and speak." This was like a red rag to a bull and just made her more determined to do it! She did listen, though, and he gave her some pointers such as typing her words in bigger print to make them easier to read.

We have always lived in the same village, so rather than just go from home to the church we decided Liam should have one last little tour around the village, past all the places that had been part of his life. The route went past Rob's house, past his best friend's house, past where he used to work, and past the schools that he went to. We told his head of year that he was going to be coming past his secondary school and he had all the kids standing outside. I told a few people that I wanted the hearse to stop just outside Liam's first school and we would like some people to walk all together to the church. I didn't want Liam arriving on his own. I was hoping for a handful of people but in the event about 200 people were outside the school waiting to walk down with us, including Liam's girlfriend Bryony.

He was buried at the local cemetery. I visit his grave by myself; we rarely go all together but it will be his birthday soon and we are all going together - although I dare say we will all still make our own individual visits! I don't need to go there to think about him but it is a beautiful cemetery, very quiet, small and intimate and focuses your mind on things. There I can be a bit more reflective. I used to go every day but now probably go every two or three days.

I didn't take down the condolence cards for months and months because looking at them made me think of all the people who were thinking of us. I did take them down eventually - bit by bit when the time was right for me. Liam's room is still as it was. Rob often says it doesn't feel like his room. We do use it - but we haven't got rid of any of his things.

I still find it really hard to write things without his name on it. I can't send birthday cards without putting his name on, and struggle that people send Christmas cards to us without his name. Just because he isn't here doesn't mean he's not a part of it any more. He is still part of the family. I talk to him all the time and feel him, but the longer it goes on the harder it gets in some respects. My most recent photograph of Liam is now two years old.

Feathers have an importance - if I see a white feather I think of him. Certain music is very important too - there was a track on a Savage Garden CD that Liam loved and we played it at his funeral. I hadn't heard it for months, then Chris and Dan had a football cup final a month ago and that tune was played. I said to myself, "Liam's here".

Fundraising has kept Liam's name in the forefront. We talk about him a lot anyway and people often say that because we talk about him, it gives them permission to talk about him too. I don't have a problem with people who have crossed the road to avoid me - they are all people who we are not necessarily that close to anyway. But a couple of people who I considered good friends have said, "I couldn't see you, it was just too hard." If they think it is hard for them, what do they think it is like for us? You do learn a lot about people in a situation like this. I find myself less tolerant of things. One of Liam's favourite programmes was Top Gear. Jeremy Clarkson recently made some flippant remarks about Richard Hammond's accident. I was incensed by his comments and wrote to him.

Christmas, mothers' day, father's day are all like a double-edged sword. I still have Amy and the boys who do lovely things for me; on Mother's day I have lovely cards, it is a very positive thing but at the same time it is negative because Liam's not there. It's always a bit of a struggle. Parts of the day I can think "This is lovely" and really enjoy it, but parts of the day are just horrible.

After Liam's death, somewhere in my head I knew that I would never ever be able to get through this by myself and I knew Rob wouldn't either. I wanted somebody else to tell me that what I was doing was OK. Hearing it from friends and family helped, but I kept thinking, "How do they know - they have no experience?" The fact that CBC could tell me that what we were doing was positive, I needed to hear that. It also helped to identify things to watch out for with the kids. With me it was more a need to hear than a need to talk, although I know it is different with everyone.

How do I view the future? I just try to deal with each thing at the time that it happens. In life there are going to be huge hurdles to get over like birthdays and Christmas which will never be the same. All the way along the line are little hurdles that trip you up when you haven't even given it a thought. I had been dieting and had to go to get weighed at a particular time on a particular day. It was snowing. I had felt really anxious all day. I got in the car to go to get weighed and was a complete wreck when I got there. I couldn't understand why until I spoke to the person weighing me. The last time I had driven in snow it was to pick up Liam and I'd gone almost the same route. Things hit you when you least expect it. The future is too scary. Chris and Dan will be 17 in November and they will be learning to drive.

It's like a part of you dies. As a mother, when you've given birth to someone, you have that connection. You get over the huge shock but you never get over the fact that you have lost your child. I hate the expression "time is a great healer". It isn't – you just learn how to live every day. But I'm a 'glass half-full' type of person. I say to people now – Liam doesn't have the opportunity to do anything any more so I am not going to squander any opportunity. I just feel sad that he isn't going to enjoy it with me.

Clare Logue

At the time of Liam's death Amy was 21, Chris and Dan 15.

He was a loving, caring, great brother. He could talk for hours about cars, reeling off the latest intricate details about how everything worked. He was never the most academic person. He never seemed to take much in, but as soon as he was reading a book on cars, that was pretty much it. He could repeat the whole book practically word by word. He just loved working on his mini and he loved being at college.

He was just lovely. If there was any sign of trouble he would walk away; he never used to get involved. He took everything at face value and never judged people. He would talk to anyone, no matter how old.

He was funny and nice and just liked everybody. We remember the stuff he used to say. He had sayings like "Look...a badger with a gun", "Cool Beans" and "Yoohoo!" when he came in.

Chris and Dan

When I heard Liam was dead, I couldn't believe it. I tried to tell myself that it isn't him, but in my heart I knew it was. I just wanted to be sick; I felt I had a big hole in my stomach.

I tend not to talk about it in front of Mum and Dad in case it upsets them. If they're upset and want to talk, then I talk but I won't initiate it. I think sometimes I've been quite snappy with them if I'm having a bad day; it's either that or burst into tears.

90

The funeral was a busy day; it's all a bit of a blur. I did the family tribute. It was really quite long as we all tried to put a memory in there, something that was special. It was really difficult but I'm glad I did it because the boys and Dad were pallbearers and Mum had done her reading at the beginning. I still think about him every day and I go up and see him at the cemetery as much as I can.

Since his death, we've spent a lot of time together as a family. We've been quite close and that's helped. We've just got lovely people around us. We're all coping with it in different ways.

Amy

91

Rose Markwort

2 April 2007

Rose

What a breeze! My pregnancy was fabulous. Physically I felt great, with no tiredness and no sickness. We were very excited and had a working title of 'Denzel' for the baby. We were a little cautious about tempting fate, so didn't buy a thing until after Xmas when I was at least 26 weeks pregnant. The nursery came together and looked lovely, peaceful. I was so happy with life and felt I was walking on air, excited about the future and the three of us.

I left work at 35 weeks and quickly got into a routine of cleaning, baking and visiting friends and family. Time went very quickly. I slowly bought toiletries and bits for the imminent birth and packed my bag. Even Matt bought himself a change bag which he was going to use when he took Denzel out. My Mum commented that she had never seen a couple so happy and excited about a new arrival and so together.

Everything is easy with hindsight but over the weekend of the 24th March I felt irritable and tired, which was unusual. I'd had some bad nights but we had learned about this in our NCT class and put it down as a sign that things were going to happen. Nothing did of course. I went to the midwife for a routine check up on the Thursday when I was 38+1, and she thought there were signs of protein so advised us to go to the hospital. We arrived and spent the next hour hooked up to routine monitors, had blood tests, my blood pressure was monitored and all came back fine. While I was on the bed Matt & I could see Denzel moving and commented on how active he was. Looking back I don't remember feeling any more kicks after this. Often my Mum has wondered if we had got Rose out then would she have survived? But I don't feel like that. I strongly believe that things happen for a reason and if she was meant to have been born that day she would have been.

As we had dinner on Thursday night, I mentioned I had felt nothing all afternoon. We thought it was strange but as all was fine not 4 hours earlier, Denzel must just be resting. But in the morning, I just knew. Somehow my belly had dropped and wasn't the hard sticky-out thing it had been. I continued with the day hoping I was wrong and waiting for a kick, but it never came. It was 1pm when I plucked up courage to ring the midwife who told me to go straight to hospital. Matt picked me up and off we went.

Matt wouldn't believe anything was wrong – he is always positive – but I just knew, which made it so hard. We arrived at the delivery suite and a midwife showed us to a room. I was scanned and could tell there was something wrong, it just all took too long. She went off and brought back a doctor. He said he couldn't see properly with the equipment, so off he went and came back with a consultant. It was only a period of ten or so minutes, but it felt like a lifetime. All the time I knew, but just hoped I was wrong. For a minute I felt like I was in a different place watching a story on TV. I heard the words but hoped she was saying it to someone else. They left us alone and we just cried.

After a gruelling labour we saw our baby girl, not a 'Denzel'. I didn't want to see her at first, scared that there would be something wrong with her physically which could spoil my dreams of what she would have been like had she lived. After a while I did think it would be good to see her but wasn't going to hold her – again too scared of that being a bad memory when all I wanted were good memories.

Leaving hospital without her was the hardest thing we did that weekend. Leaning on Matt, I made it to the car. We watched others leaving with their babies wrapped up in blankets in their car seats. Still in shock, the tears fell.

Home and on our own, we lay awake crying for what could have been. We printed the photos of her and each of us has one in our wallets as well as in picture frames in special places at home. I have created a memory box filled with all the cards we received, scan pictures, dried flowers and the one toy I had allowed myself to buy. The box is in my study where I like to work from home. It has the best views of the garden, and I watch the squirrels play around the tree we planted in Rose's memory.

The next few weeks passed by with practical things to do, death certificates to collect, a funeral service to organise. We didn't want anyone at the service. What was the point? No-one other than our parents had seen her. We waited outside the crematorium for her coffin to arrive. It was so tiny. I managed to hold it together long enough to get inside, then I don't remember anything apart from Matt picking up the coffin and walking in with it. I like to think I am a person always in control, but not that day. I couldn't imagine a future without waterproof mascara!

We had so much support from friends and family it was all a bit overwhelming, but my biggest fear was those who would cross the road to avoid having to speak to us. It wasn't something I had to worry too much about though. My first day out was a trip to the local chemist and no sooner had we got out of the car but another car had stopped and its occupant was across the road to give us big hugs. After that I knew I would be OK.

My little niece and nephew always brought me back to earth with something profound. Thomas thought Rose would come back after Easter as that's what he had been told happened to Jesus. Olivia kept singing about Rose flying up into the sky with the birds and to this day we don't know where she got that from.

As regards professional help, we took almost everything that was offered. We both felt the same which made it easier. We thought we were coping well, so instinctively knew that we needed help. With help from the Child Bereavement Charity we better understand our own feelings and each other's. Each session adds something to our box of tricks helping to understand our grief. The hospital's Bereavement Midwife has been amazing, ringing once a week almost every week for the 30 weeks that have passed. I couldn't go to the SANDS group although we did speak; I had a block about sitting in an environment where it had happened to everyone else. I had a perception in my head it would be like sitting in an AA meeting and just couldn't do it. I know it's not like that and works well for many people, but it's just not my thing.

Rose's ashes were buried in Aylesbury in an area for children. It's a lovely spot but probably a little cluttered by our tastes. Matt's brother offered to carve us a stone for the grave, something we eagerly accepted. It is amazing, by no means traditional but just so Rose. Special.

I took the 12 weeks maternity leave before going back to work. The thought of it was far worse than the actual doing. There were those who took it on and mentioned Rose and what had happened. There are those who still have yet to speak to me at all. And surprisingly, there are those who just didn't know. If I had run off with the milkman they would have known but news like this doesn't spread. It's really very weird. I lived to work before Rose but I think the break and the loss of Rose has allowed some distance which has actually been of benefit.

At home our social life has changed. Always the entertainers and organisers, we are having a year off. We felt a little like it is other people's job to entertain us after what we have been through, but our natural tendencies are starting to come through again.

It didn't take long for us to look for a positive and what we decided was to launch a business. Not just talk about it but do it, and so 'Ruby Rose' was created and almost 6 months to the day stock arrived, the website was built and we were exhibiting at the Baby Show. It's a learning curve but for me it's a success, losing Rose has made us stronger and I intend it to continue.

Pregnant again....

I knew I had conceived again only 3 weeks into the pregnancy, which is madness. I managed to wait until 4 weeks before doing a test which was positive. It was also my birthday and the weekend before going back to work – never a dull moment! And so the emotional rollercoaster began.

It wasn't too bad at the start – I guess there was less to lose then. But now I can feel the baby move, we have seen scan pictures and heard the heartbeat – I am connecting with the baby and it makes life quite hard. I seem to be permanently tired – the pregnancy, the grieving, and work demands all take their toll. I have seen others relax around me. I must be OK now I am pregnant, after all when your favourite pair of shoes break you go out and replace them and that must be what its like. No, it's actually even harder. I have the guilt and fear: would we forget Rose? why hadn't she been given the chance to live? what happens if it's not meant to be and we lose this one?

I would like a fast forward button. The weeks seem to drag, but then when I look back they have gone quite quickly. How many times have I said "It's still early days" and how many people have asked me if I would like a girl or a boy? I feel like screaming, "Anything, just a live one would do me fine."

95

We haven't and we will not be buying a thing until Denzel Junior is born. Our friends are pregnant and are happy to book flights for their new baby, not something we can bring ourselves to do although we know the act of booking a flight can have no effect on this baby's health. The pram and bits are in the loft and will remain so, the nursery curtains have never been hemmed and will not be done until after the baby is born. I know it's mad, but it's my way of coping. I finish work in 12 weeks, three of which I am on annual leave. It has come round quickly and I am doing OK.

My thoughts are moving to Rose's anniversary already. It's the first one and like every first time event, I have a wobble. I want to turn it into a family day, a celebration, but we will see – maybe the second anniversary. The 2nd April and Rose will forever be remembered in my heart.

Sarah Markwort

In between absence
When the Sun has set,
Night falls across the land.

The roses sleep, the grass is wet,
But they all know the Sun will return.

When the roses die,
They spread their seeds.
And will once again blossom,
Showing off their radiance to the bees.

When one is lost,
Their spirit still lives,
Forever in our history,
Photos in our memories.

Though people are separated,
It will not matter,
For the love and emotion,
That we will forever keep,
Is as strong as the oceans,
And just as deep.

Alexander M

96

Matt's thoughts....

Sarah being pregnant was a really exciting time but also daunting as the reality of having someone else to provide and care for was a scary thought. 'Denzel' was in there and all the way through I enjoyed talking to Denzel and being genuinely excited about the future for all three of us. Everything was going perfectly. All the plans came together, choosing furniture for the nursery and which pram to buy. With 2 weeks to go we thought we were home and dry.

Seeing Denzel move around when we went for some checks was bizarre but exciting. That night when Sarah said that Denzel had not moved, I put it out of my mind and thought everything will be fine, nothing bad will happen. The next day, when things still were not right and we went back to find that our little girl had died, was one of the most crazy situations – almost unbelievable, How could something like this happen when all had been fine the day before? The news was shocking and almost unreal.

Losing Rose was the most traumatic thing that has ever happened to us and the hardest thing as a couple we have had to deal with. From being happy and excited and ready for the impending birth, our world was suddenly turned on its head. Something that a friend said sits with me even now. He said "you just can't plan for that!" He was right. This is the last thing you expect to happen and when it does you have planned for every outcome but this one.

As a positive person I was restorative and thought of rebuilding and getting through what we would have to, but even now the biggest upset for me is what Rose has missed out on. We can get through it, move on and have the very short but happy memories that we have, but poor Rose has lost the opportunity to have a life. She has lost the most. We will never forget Rose and never forget the happy times we had with her.

The support we gained was amazing and it was intriguing to actually see and come to terms with how other people dealt with what happened to us. Some people could confront and talk to us and confidently discuss what happened and tried to understand, whereas others could not look us in the eye. What I came to realise is that everyone has different ways of dealing with things. I accepted this quickly and learned to take all support and help in whatever form from anyone, however they offered it.

Life without Rose has been quiet and at times it is almost as if it was a bad dream and it never actually happened, but it did. We will have to live with that and can – it's poor Rose that couldn't. But she will always be a part of the family we will go on to grow and love.

Matt Markwort

On the day when the weight deadens on your shoulders
And you stumble,
May the clay dance to balance you.

And when your eyes freeze behind the grey window
And the ghost of loss gets in to you,
May a flock of colours,
Indigo, red, green, and azure blue
Come to awaken in you a meadow of delight.

When the canvas frays in the currach of thought
And a stain of ocean blackens beneath you,
May there come across the waters a path of yellow moonlight
To bring you safely home.

May the nourishment of the earth be yours,
May the clarity of light be yours,
May the fluency of the ocean be yours,
May the protection of the ancestors be yours.

And so may a slow wind work these words of love around you,
An invisible cloak to mind your life.

John O'Donohue

98

Benedict "Benny" Martin Leo May

13 August 1994 –
10 May 2007

Benny died on 10th May 2007, aged 12. He was at home alone and strangled himself with an old fashioned roller towel we had on the kitchen door. He must have wondered how many times he could twist it around his neck. He always was inquisitive, and a fiddler. The police believed at first that it could have been suicide, but I never once doubted that it was just a stupid accident.

He was a happy boy with lots of friends and a loving family. Benny was the middle child, with two older brothers (Joe, 16 and Eddie, 14) and a younger sister and brother (Anna, 10 and Jacob, 6). He suffered a bit from 'middle child syndrome', but he was just beginning to come out from Eddie's shadow and forge his own way in life. He was an intelligent boy with an interesting and often unusual way of looking at life, and a quirky sense of humour. He had a great sense of justice (partly as middle child he often felt things 'weren't fair') and was quietly rebellious.

The first sleepless night after Benny's death I thought life would never be the same again. My husband Neil and I had so often felt our lives were blessed, with five beautiful children and a fantastic relationship. I thought we could never enjoy life again. But even after a couple of days I knew that life was still good, and the world was still a beautiful place.

In spite of all the tears, we felt buoyed up by our family, friends and the community. We have always been very involved in the community; our door has always been open to various waifs and strays, and also to all the kids' friends. The whole community was there to support us. Balancing the incredible pain and sense of loss was an equally incredible love. Neil and I both felt amazing love for everyone who reached out to us at that time, and since. We had so many visitors in that first week, each new visitor bringing about a new wave of grief, but also healing in the hugs. Often we couldn't speak, but could feel the love and support communicated through a hug.

My throat hurt and my body ached from all the crying, but Neil had a much more extreme reaction – he felt as though his heart had been ripped out. Once he said in front of the children 'I can't go on. My heart is broken.' Later that day I said to him 'You mustn't say that. We have to be strong for the children.'

The children didn't seem too badly affected by Benny's death. Jacob (6) is too young to really understand that Benny will never come back. Anna was the most visibly upset, but after a couple of weeks she seemed OK, though did say that she felt guilty if she was enjoying herself. Joe and Eddie had a lot of support from their friends, and their schools were very understanding. For three evenings before the funeral we had a houseful of Benny's and the boys' friends, as we had asked them to write a tribute. In the end they wrote three pieces, which were honest, funny and revealing. I think the whole process was helpful for all the children, and it also showed our door was still open.

The funeral was amazing. We had the coffin at home in the morning so that close family and friends could say a final goodbye to Benny. We wrote letters to put in the coffin, and some friends decorated it with wild flowers. It looked beautiful. The service was a fantastic tribute to Benny's life, and everyone there felt a powerful sense of love and unity.

Neil had nearly four weeks off work, but after the first week or so I had to get back into the routine of looking after the house and home. Neil spent a lot of time alone thinking about Benny and his death, and sometimes couldn't face visitors. Sometimes I felt exhausted by the number of visitors, but generally I enjoyed seeing them, and the chance to talk about Benny and how we were all coping.

We feel as though we have joined a secret club whose members have all suffered a loss. Many are people we know well, but we had never connected to this aspect of their lives. I feel that I connect more deeply with people since Benny's death, that it is easier to talk about what really matters. I know that in the future whenever anyone suffers a loss, is diagnosed with cancer or whatever, I will talk to them about it. I know that there are no right words (before I used to worry that I didn't know what to say) but that showing your love and concern is so important.

It is only five months since Benny died. Most of the time I feel fine, that life is back to normal. This is strange, and I do wonder if I am subconsciously suppressing the grief and it will hit me harder sometime hence. I am a very positive person and live very much in the present. I accept that this is the new reality. I read that your character before bereavement has a greater influence on your grief than the facts. Maybe this is why I am still so positive. Also my relationship with Neil is still fantastic and a great source of strength.

The fact that we still have four beautiful children makes a difference. There are still six of us around the dinner table when we light a candle each evening for Benny. The dynamic between the children has changed. Benny always seemed to be in the middle of most arguments, either being taunted by Eddie or picking on Anna (natural family 'pecking order' dynamics) Eddie and Benny were incredibly close, whether listening to music together or rolling around like puppies. Now Eddie and Joe are closer, and generally all is very harmonious. Neil and I are much more demonstrative towards Joe and Eddie, who we thought had grown out of needing hugs. Neil's relationship with Eddie is now much closer. But we have lost the centre of the family, the one who could one moment be listening to gangsta rap with his older brothers, and the next be playing pirates with his younger siblings.

Recently Neil and I were talking to friends, who lost their 20-year-old son ten months ago, about the need to 'let go'. I feel that I have let go of Benny, and that is why I am coping so well after such a short time. Yet sometimes I fear I have let go too much, too early, and Benny is slipping away from me. I am definitely more fragile emotionally now; tears come very easily when listening to the news or music, or even when witnessing acts of kindness.

Many good things have come out of Benny's death, such as the healing of old rifts, the re-evaluation by many people of their lives, enabling them to put what is really important back at the centre, and the incredible feeling of love for our family, friends, community and the whole world. We will always remember Benny with love in our conversations with all who knew him, and he will live on in our hearts forever.

Lilli May

101

Our son Benny died five months ago. He was 12 years old. He was a very healthy, happy, bright boy with all his life before him. But he died in a simple tragic accident at home, when everyone was out. He strangled himself on a roller towel in our kitchen, by putting his head into it, swinging and twirling it round. He was just messing about.

For most parents the death of their child is the most awful thing they could ever imagine. When Benny died the pain was so great that I did not believe that I would be able to continue living. But I did. And I want to tell you how Benny's death has not only been about pain.

We are a lucky family in many ways. We still have four lovely children, aged 6, 10, 14 and 16. My wife and I are very close. We are surrounded by many friends and a close community. In the week following Benny's death over 150 family friends and neighbours must have visited our house. There were over 250 at Benny's funeral, held a week after he died. Very few people stayed away from us from fear or embarrassment. We were embraced by so many, we cried with so many. We experienced so much unfeigned and heartfelt love and sympathy that we were lifted up out of the deep pit of sorrow and despair, and were given hope. Not only our lives but the whole community seemed for a moment to have been transformed by love, which was Benny's gift to us through his death. And suddenly all the suffering in the world seemed to have meaning because of this. The world seemed nourished by sorrow, which breaks open the dead seeds of our closed hearts and minds to things that are really important, true and good, allowing these seeds to bring forth the fruit of life again, ten fold and a hundred fold. And no sorrow is greater than that of the death of a child.

We are lucky. But we know that many are not so lucky. How I would have coped had I had only one or two children, or if my wife and I were not close and happy, or if we were more isolated with less friends and family, I do not know. My heart goes out to all those who are less fortunate. May all who mourn be comforted.

However I think also that we were able to be lucky and to receive love and healing because of one very important part of our response to Benny's death. This was our acceptance of his death, acceptance in every part of ourselves. By this I mean that we did not try to find someone or something to blame, and nor did we try to divert the pain of the death from our selves through denials, distractions or fantasies. Not all of our family reacted in the same way. I think the older brothers were and still are in shock and that some of the pain of the wound is still to come. My wife and I have also reacted differently because I am someone who needs to ask questions, whereas Lilli does not – she is a more instinctive person. However, overall as a family we were able to receive the deep wound of Benny's death without anger or denial and without trying to dull the pain in any way. We all went to see his body in the mortuary on the day that he died. We talked with everyone openly about his death. We laid his body out in the house on the day of the funeral and all wrote letters to Benny to put in his coffin. We all stood round the coffin, holding hands and looking at his darling dead body, before the lid was fastened down and we saw him no more.

I am crying as I write this, because the pain is still so great and so deep.

For me this acceptance is not only about healing, but about knowing. When Benny died I felt that I had been cut open from head to foot, and all my insides, my body, heart, mind and soul, had been exposed. I felt Benny's death differently in the different parts of my self. For days I had physical spasms, and my body was covered in a rash. Even now my body aches for Benny's physical presence, his hug. That pain will never end. This I also have to accept. On the other hand my heart felt that it had been ripped open, and I was haemorrhaging hope and life. But now my heart feels open to so many others, I feel that it is alive in a way that it was not before. My mind was tormented with images and memories, and now is asking big questions which I know that I have to address. But my soul was always at peace, when at last I found my soul.

It was a revelation to me that there were so many different ways of knowing and feeling in the different parts of the self. This was why I could feel pain, joy and peace all at the same time. And this knowledge enabled me, after the first few weeks, not to be overwhelmed by any one feeling. I knew that somewhere in my self there was peace and hope and I did not have to hide from or deny the pain, to be able to go on.

Five months after and I am back at work in a busy job. In many ways things are back to normal, although I can break down and cry at the slightest reminder of Benny. But in some ways things will never be the same, and I don't want them to be. These things are the gifts that Benny has given to me in his death.

The first gift is that life is now real as it never was before. It is easy to wander through life in a kind of dream thinking that only you exist and nothing else matters. Benny's death cut through all this, it opened me up so that I knew once and for all that he really existed and that others really exist and that everyone and everything is precious and worthy of being loved.

The second gift is that everything has now been put in perspective, in the perspective of the love and truth we experienced through Benny's death. I still get frustrated and anxious about work, money, status and so on, but not so much as in the past. These worries are so minor, by comparison with the loss of Benny. I used to rush around madly, and didn't spend as much time with Benny or the other children as I perhaps should have done. Now I ask myself, what is really important in my life? This is not just with my family but with my work, and other activities. I am putting love and truth, in joy and peace, at the centre of my life.

Finally Benny taught me and still teaches me that I can no longer put off the question of meaning in my life. Why did Benny die, and what is he now? These are the same questions as: Why am I alive? What am I? And what is the purpose of this creation? These are not questions to be answered in logic or in words, though words may help. They have to be answered in every part of the self and in the timelessness of eternity. I must ask these questions completely seriously and without pre-conceptions, because nothing but the truth will do. I have to let go of everything, even my grief, even my love. I must give myself time for timelessness, time for my body, heart, mind and soul to ask these questions. We all need to give ourselves space to be fully human, space outside the increasing pressures, noise and continual distractions of modern living. Otherwise we will not only become less human, but also be unable to cope with ourselves, our loved ones, and our own unavoidable mortality.

I realise now that all sorrow comes from love. It is the great risk we take when we really care for others, for something beyond ourselves. It is the great price we pay for being fully human. But who would stop loving? Not me. The only way I can deal with this terrible burden of love is by seeking meaning, ultimate meaning. I already sense that this meaning exists, but Benny's death has spurred me on to put this search at the centre of my life. It is a search in both desperation and in hope. It is a search both for Benny and for my own self. It is a lifetime's work and it is also, with Benny's help, a lifetime's play. It is Benny's great gift to me and to our family. Thank you, my dear sweet lovely boy.

Neil May

104

Writings for Benny

Being opened up.
Being blinded, disabled, made idiot, struck deaf and dumb,
Dislocated from my own self, and from the world.

Crucified
Arms open in pain and longing
Arms open in acceptance.

No place to hide
No dreams to wake from
No solace that gives solace
No balm, no calm.

I feel as though life has taken a sharp serrated knife
And cut me right open, with one sure slice.

And here I am, organs and entrails,
My body, heart, mind and soul,
All my hopes, fears, and weak faith
Quivering upon the butcher's slab.

Opened up.

I am dumb as a beast.

But sometimes it feels as though an angel has come,
Cleaving the heavens, cutting through the pain,
Arriving suddenly.

So bright that I can see nothing but her radiance
So full of love and truth
That I am crying with joy
Crying with gratitude
Crying with relief
Even as I see my dear son
Dying, so unnecessarily,
But still shining
With the same angelic light,
But not total light,
Not blotting out the world,
But illuminating it.

Neil May

Writings for Benny

It is raining
God is crying
For all the sorrow in the world,
now. For all the sorrow
since time began.

And sometimes God weeps
great storms of tears,
shouting out and beating his chest
opening his broken heart to all creation.

And sometimes
he weeps gently
slowly,
tears of love and compassion,
tears which water this sad earth
in such kindness
that we are nourished by his pain.

Let it rain

Neil May

I used to play on the swing with Benny to see who could jump off the furthest. Sometimes Anna, Benny and I played pirates, it was better when he joined in. We miss him now as we have to have an imaginary crew. I felt a bit shy at the funeral but afterwards I enjoyed playing with everyone, and the nice food. I didn't like it when the younger children at school kept asking me if Benny had died. I like looking at photos of Benny and remembering him.

Jacob (6)

I have good memories of Benny like playing out in the garden with him and doing acrobatics in the living room, but often we had arguments which I'm starting to miss.

When mum and dad first told me I felt a bit sick and shocked. When we went to the hospital to see him I started to feel sad, but mainly worried because

106

mum and dad kept on crying which was very strange. I tried to distract myself and have fun but every time I did I felt slightly guilty.

Anna (10)

Benny was someone I could have a joke with and chill out with. We also used to fight but we would always make up afterwards. On the night before he died we had an argument and then I said that I wouldn't stick up for him in a fight, but now I know that I would.

The police came into the school to tell me that Benny had died and I just felt numb.

My family was very, very upset at first but now they are calmer - but I think they are still upset and will never recover from it. I think I am still in shock and it will come to me gradually that I will never see him again.

Eddie (14)

Benny was a really lively boy who cared a lot about what he did. He was still quite childish in some ways, because he liked playing with Anna and Jacob, but was grown up in other ways. At home I wasn't particularly close to him as he was just one of the family, but I miss him now.

At first I was really shocked and nothing seemed interesting or fun. But I didn't feel particularly tearful, just a bit numb. At the moment I think that I will never stop feeling sad from time to time, but that life will gradually get easier, and I will end up just feeling sad because such a lovely person isn't still living, rather than feeling sad about the death itself, and sad for myself.

Joe (16)

107

Rosie Mayling

17 December 1991 –
14 May 2003

Rosie

Rosie our eleven-year-old daughter had been ill and in hospital with Vasculitis for two and a half months. It was a horribly traumatic, stressful time. While I was sleeping in a camp bed beside Rosie, David would be desperately trying to juggle looking after Ellie, our older daughter, and battling the M40 sometimes four times daily.

There was neither emotional nor physical support for families during our hospital stay and the strains for all of us were intolerable. Eventually Rosie's consultants at Oxford reached a diagnosis but none of us ever considered that she would not recover. When she was discharged at last we were all hopeful that she would soon return to school. She was desperate to see her friends and had completed all her schoolwork which her teachers had sent in for her. She asked "Mummy, when will I be better and be able to go back to Redroofs?" She loved her school. I told her that it would be very soon. We really did think it would be. While we were on our way home from the hospital my mum had been to our home and draped welcome home banners around and there was a bottle of pink sparkling champagne waiting for us. We thought the worst was over. It was such a happy day.

Rosie was home for just six days when, early on the morning of Bank Holiday Monday May 6th 2003, she suffered a massive pulmonary haemorrhage followed by a cardiac arrest and spent the next nine days in intensive care on a ventilator at the John Radcliffe hospital. It is hard to remember much about the next nine days but what I do recall is the feeling of helplessness, horror, isolation and fear like nothing else I had ever imagined. When the decision was made to switch off the life support machine, the devastation was beyond belief. On May 14th 2003 we had to say goodbye to our beautiful, clever, talented, cheeky, caring and beloved Rosie - not just for a while but forever.

The death of a child is the most painful experience any family can suffer. It is beyond the realms of most people's imagination. There is no word to describe the pain. Well meaning people say, "I just can't imagine!" The answer I give is, "No you cannot, and I would not want you to!"

I remember that afternoon, just an hour afterwards being directed out of PICU down the corridor to see the bereavement counsellor. We stumbled alone to an office where a well meaning lady gave David and I a cup of weak tea, a pile of leaflets on how to register a child's death and said she was sorry! I do not know quite what we were expecting as we were totally numb and in a state of shock, but with little practical and no emotional support we were despatched twenty minutes later and left to drive home and get on with it. Two days later, David suffered a heart attack due entirely to the intolerable stress of the last few months.

David came home from hospital saying he wished he had not come through the heart attack and we staggered through the funeral .So here we were with a family of three instead of four and a huge, ugly, gaping void in our life instead of a cheeky, loving, chatty little girl.... and now what? Our entire family were totally lost, shocked and in despair, and the full horror of living without the child we loved most in the whole world was just beginning to hit us like a tidal wave.

In the immediate aftermath, our house was full of well meaning friends and family. There were flowers everywhere. Friends of Rosie sent letters, cards. Our elder daughter Ellie's best friend set up a little website called "Memories of Rosie" and for several months, all her friends and her family posted hundreds of messages regularly on the site. There were poems, anecdotes, letters of support and love and this really was a lifesaver. Gradually over the next few weeks, the silence set in. The house emptied out, the flowers died, and people returned to their normal lives.

Ellie returned to school. It was a terrible time for her. I still wonder how she managed to cope when her parents were torn apart and her normal safe life as she knew it was gone forever. She was fourteen and was so close to Rosie.

She was dealing with GCSE pressures on top of trying to wade through the grief. Ellie was also a full time pupil at Redroofs Theatre School, which is our family business. The loss of Rosie had hit the school very hard, but everyone was brilliant and looked after Ellie as best they could.

We contacted the Child Bereavement Charity and for the first time we felt supported with practical advice and compassion. We felt a little safer in the knowledge that here was someone who knew how to help us and at that point it was our lifeline. They put me in touch with a really good counsellor and I found out subsequently that the CBC had initiated and set up this much needed counselling post. In the long lonely months following, I attended weekly bereavement counselling and attended some CBC bereavement support groups where we were introduced to other parents. It slowly dawned on me that there are so many other people who have lost their children, that the world is not only made up of warm cosy complete families to whom bad things do not happen. The worst can and does happen to anyone! Here right on my doorstep were so many other families who were also crying out for support. Nobody can make it better or take away the pain, but knowing we were not the only ones helped us to keep sane.

We really wanted to give something back. Ellie, who is multi-talented, together with her best friend composed a beautiful song called "Rainbows Light" which was picked up and recorded by Chris Eaton who is a producer for Sir Cliff Richard. Ellie decided that the proceeds from her CD would go to the CBC. David and I subsequently took part in a film called "A Loss Too Soon" which is used in training courses run by the CBC for healthcare and other professionals.

One day the "Memories of Rosie" website crashed and when it was fixed some weeks later, it seemed that most of our support network of friends had forgotten about the site or chose not to revisit because it was time to "move on". It was a natural progression and it had to happen but the emptiness and pain for us, Rosie's family, who could never "move on" was impossible to describe.

I now treasure the few close friends who walk beside us all the way. Some fell by the wayside – well, who can blame them? It's not an easy job! I realised at this time that really and truly the only way to stay sane and survive this horror was to be pro-active and to help myself. It was a lonely revelation and there were several coping strategies which gradually began to evolve.

One day my sister told me about a website called Compassionate Friends. Her friend in America had a brother who was murdered and her parents had found this useful. I logged on to this site, which offers support and friendship and is run by and for bereaved parents. Through the website I met the most supportive group of bereaved parents without whom I don't think I could have coped. I met other 'mums' who would be there for me in the dead of night when I was a tearful wreck, unable to sleep and experiencing frightening flashbacks and they offered compassion and understanding and were there for me often till two in the morning. These women remain true and treasured friends.

I discovered Reiki which is a form of spiritual healing. I attended courses and qualified as a Reiki practitioner. I found this really helpful and use this occasionally on friends but mostly on myself as a way of calming myself down when I'm having a particularly bad day. It restores a measure of control which was one of the things which I feel had been ripped from me. As a person who has always been in control of my life, the loss of Rosie made me realise that in reality, although we may con ourselves into believing we are in control , no matter how much you plan and think you have life down to a fine art it can and does change within a nano-second. Reiki fuelled my growing interest in all things spiritual and I regularly attend the comforting local spiritualist church.

Shortly after Rosie's death we set up our registered charity, Rosie's Rainbow Fund (www.rosiesrainbowfund.co.uk). The focus required for running our charity has been considerable and it is my way of honouring my beautiful daughter. When I carry out my work with Rosie's Rainbow Fund, I feel that not only is Rosie driving me forward to achieve amazing and positive things to help other sick children and their families, but it's also Rosie's way of making sure I am able to survive. It has been the most powerful coping tool of all and has opened up paths I never knew existed. In helping others who are experiencing pain it is a distraction from my own.

I went back to dance teaching after four months. Running a busy theatre school has been great for keeping me firmly in the "now". Of course it's been very difficult at times and learning to cope with working with children, many of whom were Rosie's classmates, has been a challenge but I think I manage pretty well. The kids are fantastic and I love my business and running the school. Each year the children and students form the Rosie's Rainbow Choir and we tour all over the place at Christmas spreading the word of the Fund. In this way I make sure Rosie stays centre stage as she always was.

I have learnt that everyone grieves differently. In the early days I thought that my husband and older daughter would need what I did and often battled with them to find a counsellor because watching their suffering is even worse than dealing with my own. I tried to help them by doing things I thought helpful, but it simply didn't work. I have had to back down and let them find their own way. David does his grief work by working out in the gym. Ellie for a time threw herself into music, composing some extraordinary songs. Nowadays, I feel she locks it away and that one day perhaps she will seek professional help if she needs to, but for now she is coping and is strong and brave and a wonderful person. She is throwing herself into dance college life, which she loves. I feel in awe of the way she has coped with the loss of her soul sister and I am immensely proud of her.

Living in our old house had too many memories. Rosie's room stayed virtually unchanged. David would go in there and talk to her but I couldn't go in there. Having to pass her room and turn my head away every time I went upstairs became a nightmare. Despite David's misgivings and fear of "leaving Rosie behind", we packed her things and moved house. He now agrees this was helpful and we have no regrets.

About three months after we lost Rosie I began to write and write and write. Over the past four years I have written hundreds of pages, documenting not only day to day happenings of my new life without Rosie but also the anger and pain, my almost suicidal thoughts at very black low times. Tapping my innermost thoughts into my computer is immensely cathartic and this has manifested itself into the writing of a book about this impossible journey. I don't know whether anyone will ever publish it or even whether the often difficult content would make suitable reading. But it exists now in black and white. My 'book' is now turning into something like "War and Peace" and I don't know where the journey's end is because grief has no end. It goes on and we learn to smile again and we get better "at" it but that is as good as it gets. However, I sometimes read back over my early writings and note with amazement how, despite all odds, my family and I are moving through this and can see how, imperceptibly, little chinks of light are showing themselves through the darkness. Through a tragedy which rocked the foundations of every facet of our life I can see that, like it or not, we are learning to live again without Rosie.

Carolyn Mayling

112

Annabelle Alice McCabe

15th March 2006

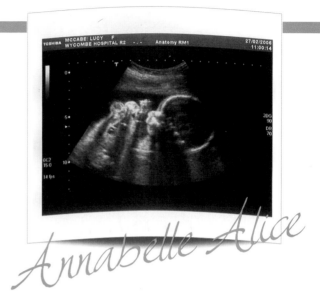

Annabelle Alice

After two years of unsuccessfully trying for a baby and knowing that I had endometriosis, we made the difficult decision to embark on a cycle of IVF. I was full of hope, excitement and fear, but convinced that I would soon be round and happy.

Another two years and four fresh cycles later, however, all we were left with was empty arms and pockets, with our hopes and dreams teetering very near the edge of despair. Thinking about our future was almost too much to bear and a big black infertility cloud had started to follow my every move. Determined to draw a line under this chapter we approached a new forward thinking clinic. Some very expensive blood tests later I was given a possible, albeit controversial, reason for my infertility and with renewed hope got back on the roller coaster for round 5. The treatment was gruelling, but imagine our joy at my first ever positive pregnancy test and the utter shock when early scans revealed triplets – identical twins and a fraternal triplet!

The twins were fine with hearts beating away but the triplet was much further behind. Sadly, "twinkle" didn't make it. But at last I was on my way to the 'happy ending' that so many others had realised and, along with all my friends and family who had watched helplessly over the last four years, was buzzing with happiness. I'd persevered and done it and was so proud I wanted to shout from the roof tops. However, I had another routine scan the day before Christmas Eve and was dealt the devastating blow that the twins had died – just like that. The sadness and tears were excruciating and of course the big

113

black cloud returned. I never realised life could be so bad. I had some frozen embryos and one month later embarked on a frozen cycle which although not as gruelling resulted in another negative.

I was a physical wreck for cycle number 7 and my heart was truly in my mouth the day I received the call to say I was pregnant again. The big black cloud slipped away and the ecstasy and relief were indescribable, if short lived as I endured 12 weeks of nerve-wracking repeat pregnancy tests, scans and thrice daily injections. Nevertheless, I made it to my 12 week scan which was just magical and passed in a complete dream, and finally I had those prized photographs of my baby which clearly showed that he/she had my nose! Christmas 2005 was perfect and at last I was admitted to that longed-for 'members only club' and entered a whole new world where I was allowed to discuss antenatal appointments, prams, baby names, schooling, cribs, cots, nursery designs...

As time went on all thoughts I'd had about what I would do if I ever got pregnant, of going private and opting for a caesarean, dissipated as I wanted and began to feel like a normal Mum. I grew lovely and round and often snuck to the toilet at work to look at my profile! Everywhere I went, I revelled in the fact that I was the pregnant woman drinking orange juice and wearing maternity jeans. We were even fitted for a maternity bridesmaid's dress! Each night I "spoke" to my baby about what we were going to do together, what weddings and parties we had been invited to and of course what we were going to wear. I even felt able to voice my preference for a little girl, although of course a little boy would have been just as wonderful.

This baby changed our life beyond recognition and was suddenly the centre of our universe. Every thought, plan and dream included him/her and when the kicks started I was beside myself with joy and often got into positions to feel their full effect. My anomaly scan was late due to non-existent antenatal care, but I enjoyed every second of watching my baby "drink its elevenses" with the most enormous tongue! To our huge relief everything was fine and to our intense delight we found out that we were having a lovely little girl. The grins were fixed firmly on our faces and I could tell that Neil finally relaxed and was absolutely over the moon. We went home in a halo of happiness and stopping to do some food shopping on the way seemed like the best experience of my life. Over the next few days Annabelle Alice kept coming to mind as a name for our child.

Ten days later I had not felt any movement for nearly a whole day and Neil suggested a trip to the hospital to get some reassurance. Thinking that I would be given a pat on the head and sent home, I was surprised at how seriously I was taken and ushered to a side ward. The midwife was unsuccessful in locating the baby's heartbeat with a Doppler but claimed the machine was broken. I was anxious but not unduly worried and waited for the scanner to be brought down from another floor. I cannot remember the words that were spoken to let me know that Annabelle had died, but can remember feeling utterly wretched and crying out. We were left alone to try and take in what had happened and I climbed onto Neil's lap and cried.

It was Saturday night and the consultant was called from home. He was very kind and talked through what would happen next and described how Annabelle's skin would be thinner than a normal new born as she was so early. It was utterly incomprehensible to me that I would have to give birth and I begged for a caesarean but was told that this was impossible and that one day I would be thankful. I was given drugs to start the induction process, and we were told to go home and come to terms with what had happened, and come back 48 hours later. And so began the texting and phoning of hundreds of family and friends to let them know our daughter had died. How could this have happened to us? Telling our Mums and Dad was desperate.

The next day my parents and brothers and sisters arrived as I was changing our bed, that nesting instinct still going strong. Within hours the terror of having to give birth had abated and I was ready and calm about what was to come, but for Neil and my family it was horrific and I remember my sister trying to encourage me to eat and keep my strength up for labour. Cheated out of the excitement of preparing a bag with baby clothes and unwrapping a new car seat, I borrowed some slippers and one of Neil's shirts and drove to the hospital. Labour was five short hours, just as my Mum and Grandmother had experienced, and painful. But I wish it had gone on forever and would not have had a caesarean for the world.

Stating Annabelle was lovely doesn't even come close, and she did indeed have my nose! Her resemblance to a great aunt who had passed away and not been thought about for many years was uncanny. High with hormones about what I had achieved, I rang and texted friends just like any new Mum who has finally met her child. I hadn't bought any baby things so she was wrapped in a hospital blanket. Why, oh why hadn't I taken a new blanket and with it the opportunity to do at least one thing for my daughter? But I had put two small matching wooden teddies in her room weeks earlier and placed one by her side as I held her for the first and last time. Leaving her tore my heart apart.

About two weeks later we left the house for the first time. Due to even more terrible post-natal care I haemorrhaged and lost around four pints of blood at a service station on the M1. I was taken by Ambulance to A&E and spent a terrifying day without being given any indication of what was happening and thinking that I was about to lose my womb. Eventually I was rushed to theatre and spent another two days on a labour ward being transfused. I didn't lose my womb and have since learnt that premature babies often cause haemorrhage due to retained pieces of placenta.

We opted for an autopsy and Annabelle's funeral was delayed. Time passed in a blur. I almost forgot that it was going to happen, didn't ask anyone and was distraught that we didn't have the usual favourite song, poem, book or saying from our short time together to play or read. I had, however, preserved my Winnie the Pooh books and photocopied a favourite poem that I knew she would have been read over and over again. The morning of the funeral we went to our local florist and I struggled over the right flowers. I chose some Arum Lilies, cut short and tied with raffia, and bought a white balloon. Unable to hold back the tears, I began to sob. A nice lady in the shop asked if I, like her, had lost a child – it seems that others who have experienced the same just know. We were very early and went to a nearby coffee shop. How absurd it felt to be drinking tea waiting to go to our daughter's funeral while everyone around us fussed over their babies.

Finally the time came and we nervously entered the Crematorium not knowing what to do or say, but the undertaker met us with a small white coffin. He passed it to Neil and the tears started and wouldn't stop. We went through the motions and laid our poem and flowers and left. Suddenly on the way home I 'woke up' to the fact that I wanted to involve our parents. I made a call to ask if we could all let the balloon go around Dad's pond where I am sure that Annabelle would have spent hours looking for frogs just like her cousins – but Dad was at work and once again I felt I'd failed Annabelle by not even organising a "proper" funeral although we did go to the pond the next day, albeit with a much deflated balloon!

I don't like to fuss but in an attempt to do something I had some cards printed with Annabelle's hand and foot prints and sent them to our family. Although

116

I now sense this wasn't enough for Nannies and Granddads, Aunties and Uncles, and am greatly distressed by not knowing what else I can do, particularly for my Mum. We at least have a few precious memories but she had to carefully ask to see a picture of Annabelle. And I know that in a way Mum hurts more than us, as she is hurting for me as well as for herself.

We collected Annabelle's ashes but have never been able to part with them. Instead they sit high on a shelf in our bedroom with the other teddy, providing strange comfort, and I'm very sure I won't ever let her go again. The physical feeling of not having her inside me cut like a knife and I couldn't go to sleep at night because I didn't want to wake up and remember that she was gone. I cried every day for six months but gradually the days between sobbing did become less and less.

The door closed quickly on the 'member's only club', I went through the agony of swiftly being fitted for a new bridesmaid's dress and the big black cloud returned. I felt so shut out, desolate and lonely walking around in my own little bubble of sadness. Just like any new Mum, using her name was new territory and seemed slightly odd but has never really moved on for me, besides she was never to be Annabelle. I liked the formality of the name but was 100% sure that it would be shortened and Annabelle has so many wonderful possibilities – Annie, Bella, Be, Ella, Bebe, Annie Be Be – but it was not to be and oddly she has become an even more formal Annabelle Alice.

Coming home also provoked some feelings I had never experienced before like stomach churning terror at meeting anyone I knew and not wanting to leave the house even for one night. Going about normal life seemed ridiculous. How could I be pushing a trolley round the supermarket when all I wanted to do was scream "did you know my little girl died"? But what else was there to do.

Not being in the right mind I didn't take my maternity leave and going back to an office that wasn't the friendliest of places anyway was extremely tough. People were split into a mixture of head down, confusion – wasn't she pregnant last time I saw her? – and still to this day I bump into people who ask how my little one is.

I am getting better at saying I had a little girl but she died – a few little words that hurt so much but others can't quite comprehend and, judging by the responses, often think they've misheard or don't quite believe you.

117

Looking at her photograph just stuns. I didn't want this to have happened – not just the obviousness of losing Annabelle but having had something so terrible happen. I'd had an idyllic childhood and life so far and didn't want this to change me, to be someone with sadness in their life. But I took great solace from the words of another bereaved mum: "Life is not better, life is not worse, it's just different". A year and a half later it's probably somewhat correct although there are still many agonising moments and lots of expected but also unexpected tears. I don't feel that I lost Annabelle Alice as she is a part of me and every thought I take and every move I make, but she's missing, missing from every moment.

Now every invitation, plan, Christmas or birthday makes my heart jump and I've gone from an A1 planner and organiser to sitting on the back bench. Going to events or places without Annabelle, or wishing with all my heart that I will be pregnant again "by then" and knowing how disappointed I will be if I'm not, is hard. But we go to the weddings and parties and quietly join in while other babies are announced, introduced, loved and cooed over. Our relationship hasn't faltered and we go about our daily business, but life is on hold and we are tethered while we wait.

Over time others forget. I love talking about her but it can cause embarrassment or dismissiveness. Some close friends are wonderful in letting me join in their stories of pregnancy, labour and birth but I never feel that I am really "allowed" to share mine, and for others it makes for very uncomfortable listening. One was shocked that I named "her" and some believe she was born by osmosis. I feel like I'm causing a scene, justifying, showing off almost, when I try and explain otherwise. The mothers of children that I religiously buy birthday and Christmas presents for have no way to remember Annabelle's birthday. But I will never forget – and the most wonderful thing is feeling that it is the most natural thing in the world to sign every Christmas card, every birthday card, every letter with three kisses: one from me, one from Neil and one with a dotted halo from Annabelle Alice.

I wish. I wish I could have known you better. I wish I could protect, cherish and care for you. I wish I could show you to the world. I wish we could laugh and play together.

We never did get an answer as to why Annabelle died. We embarked on another – disastrous – round of IVF six months later, which produced a negative result.

Lucy McCabe

118

Mary Caitlin Neill

12th May 1996 –
6th January 1998

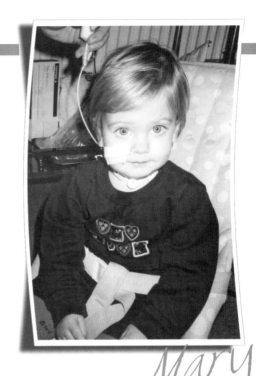

Mary

Mary was born on Sunday 12th May and weighed 8lb 3oz – heavier than both her sisters, Rosie (1992) and Nancy (1994). The first six months of Mary's life were happy and healthy. She was gaining weight and was always such a happy and sunny-natured baby.

November 1996 was when the problems began. Mary developed a pronounced stridor (gasping for breath) after having had a cold/chest infection. Initially we were told it was croup but as Mary made no improvement, eventually the ENT consultant performed a laryngoscopy; this resulted in his diagnosis of Laryngo-Malacia – a 'floppy larynx' - which we were told she would grow out of and not to worry.

The next few months were very difficult. Mary slowly lost more and more weight as she tired from her struggle to breathe. She was refusing solids and became increasingly frail. As her resistance was lowered, she continually contracted various infections and Mary was constantly at the GP's for antibiotics. We had been told not to worry but this was becoming an increasingly impossible task.

119

Eventually, during February 1997 we were referred back to the local ENT consultant; this led to a referral to Great Ormond Street as the situation was now critical and we could no longer presume the original diagnosis was correct. Once at GOSH another laryngoscopy was performed in March 1997.

What followed was a terrible shock for us. We learned that Mary had vocal chord palsy; due to their inability to move, her vocal chords were in a stationary semi-open position and this was the cause of her breathing obstruction. We were told it was necessary for her to have a tracheostomy in order to survive. Despite our shock and worry we knew Mary had no alternative. Various neurological tests were done at this stage to see if a reason could be found for the vocal chord palsy but nothing was detected. We were at GOSH for a month during which time the operation was performed, Mary became strong enough to return home and Simon and I were taught all the skills needed to manage Mary's tracheostomy at home.

Rosie and Nancy coped so well throughout the whole of Mary's illness. They never resented the time I was away from them. They enjoyed their visits to GOSH and their sheer devotion and love for their little sister was so apparent all through. Due to wonderful family support, both Simon and I were able to be with Mary at all times; we never wanted to leave her alone without either one of us.

Once home again, we learnt surprisingly quickly to adjust to life with the trachy. It was of course very difficult and we were so lucky to be given a full-time health care assistant to help during the week. She turned out to be a gift from heaven; she was so devoted to Mary, the girls and all of our family. Her help was invaluable and she remains to this day a dear and treasured friend. We were now feeding Mary with the nasogastric tube hoping that over time this would help her to gain weight and eventually she would be able to feed orally again.

During September 1997 however, Mary began to develop other problems. She began to have difficulty swallowing and would often 'aspirate' into her trachy tube. She also began to get terribly sick after feeding. This was a very difficult time and caused her much discomfort. It was also a very anxious time for us as each time Mary aspirated into her trachy tube this caused a potentially life-threatening situation for her.

Eventually things became too difficult for us to manage at home. I felt there were underlying problems to Mary's condition that we had not got to the bottom of as yet. It was a battle, but eventually we got Mary re-referred to GOSH and demanded for more investigative tests to be done.

These resulted in the discovery that Mary was suffering from severe oesophageal reflux due to a weak stomach valve. We were told she would need surgery to improve this. The Paediatric Neurologist repeated the very painful neurological tests which Mary had had the previous March, but which had failed to show up anything significant at that time.

The greatest shock of all came when Simon and I were told by the neurologist that, as a result of these latest tests, he feared that Mary had a very rare and progressive genetic disorder called 'Fazio-Londe Disease'. We were also told that, if this was correct, she would not live beyond the age of two. We were totally devastated. The neurologist said he would re-do the tests in February when he could be even more certain, but the outlook was extremely bleak. Mary then underwent an operation to have a gastrostomy tube fitted. This improved the quality of the last part of her life as the sickness had been causing her great discomfort and distress. We returned home.

Tragically, we were never able to get the tests repeated as Mary contracted a virus over Christmas 1997 and we had to go back into Wycombe Hospital. The virus developed rapidly into pneumonia and after a week in hospital, Mary died peacefully in my arms on Tuesday 6th January 1998.

As the neurologist had explained to us just six weeks before, the nature of this progressive disorder would mean that more and more of Mary's muscles would weaken and eventually when her respiratory muscles were affected, it would be likely that she would be unable to fight off a respiratory infection. This is exactly what happened, but it happened so much sooner than we had expected. It was also very hard for us as we had been waiting for the neurologist to do follow-up tests to confirm the diagnosis so we also had to cope with the anxiety of not knowing whether or not he was right. Of course, eventually we had to accept that he was correct.

Although Mary's life had been so difficult for her and she had had so much to cope with, she was such a happy and caring little girl. She adored Rosie and Nancy and all of us. She showed us all that 'love is all you need' and if you have love you can cope with anything. We all miss Mary terribly.

Following her death, we talked about her constantly. We had to accept that she is still with us but in a very different way; she is in our hearts. I do believe she is where she needs to be on her spiritual journey and I always gain great comfort from talking to her whenever the pain becomes too great to bear. She changed our lives. As the years have passed since Mary's death the pain will always be there but it has become a part of us, a part we have had to learn to manage and carry with us.

At the time of Mary's death Simon and I were able to support each other and our relationship gave us the strength to help us to cope. Although we had always had difficulties in our marriage, it felt as if our shared grief for Mary brought us closer together at this time. I could never have imagined not sharing my life with him, as he was the only other person who felt the same intensity of love and grief for my darling Mary.

However as the years have slipped by we found our grief did take us on continually widening paths and the different ways we found to cope with our grief caused the difficulties in our marriage to intensify and grow. After trying our very hardest to sort things out and hold onto our marriage, sadly, we both had to agree that the only and most positive way forward for us all as a family was to separate in September 2005.

Although the last two years have not been easy ones, Simon and I have remained, and I believe always will remain the best of friends – we share the most precious gift life can offer; that of our three beautiful daughters, and nothing will ever change that. I believe nothing can ever sever the intensity of the bonds of love between family members, not the end of a marriage, not even death.

Mary will be with us always.

'All is well'.

Karen Neill

James Aidan Pearson

21 March 2007

On September 6th 1995 I married David, a widower, and became a stepmother to his three small children, Andrew aged 6, Michael aged 4 and Holly aged 2. Having grown up in a large family I was unfazed by the challenge of instant motherhood.

From the beginning I was keen to have a baby, which I felt would help to unite us together as a new family; David was less keen, feeling that his family was complete, but reluctantly agreed. I was 31 yrs old.

Months came and went. Years came and went. No baby. A constant roller-coaster of hope and quiet disappointment. By the time I was 40 in 2004 I had given up and began to re-define the kind of future I would look forward to.

It came as a huge shock therefore when I found myself pregnant in December 2006. I was terrified, alarmed and elated all at the same time. David shared some of these emotions, but with the news coming just weeks before his 50th birthday, had great reservations about starting all over again. It was a time of very mixed emotions.

We stumbled through the lead up to Christmas trying to carry on as normal. On Christmas day, just as I was about to collect friends who were spending the day with us, I noticed some bleeding. Panic stricken, I had to give the

123

performance of my life and behave as if all was well with the world. I knew then just how much this baby meant to me. By Boxing Day morning I was distraught. I rang my friend Marion and she came straight round; she was calm, reassuring and encouraging. I saw my GP the next day and she referred me for an early scan. Pregnant herself, she assured me that bleeding was not unusual and to try to be positive. By this time I had told my sisters and one of them, Theresa, flew over from Ireland to accompany me to the scan.

I saw my baby for the first time that day. There was an unmistakeable heartbeat. All was well. My heart soared! I began to let myself believe that it might just happen for me...

Over the next two months there were a few ups and downs; a blood test abnormality leading to some more tests, scans in London, a possible diabetes scare but eventually everything settled down and we began to relax and plan our loft conversion, which would accommodate an expanding family. My bedtime reading was dominated by pregnancy and baby books, fuelling my excitement.

In mid March, David and I flew to Ireland for my niece's wedding. The next day was Mother's Day. I spent the day with my elderly mother and the evening with my lovely teenage children. It was certainly the most special Mothers Day I'd ever had. I was a mother. A real mother. I felt blessed and privileged.

Sadly, only 24 hours later I experienced what I now know to be a premature rupture of membranes. I was 19 weeks pregnant.

I didn't know what had happened. I thought I had developed a urinary tract infection. It was late evening and David was getting ready for a skiing trip in the morning. I went to bed and had decided to ring the midwife in the morning. I often marvel now at just how naive I was. I have been a nurse for almost 25 years.

The midwife listened to my tale, was too busy to fit me in and although she encouraged me to make an appointment with my GP, she gave me no grounds for concern even when I mentioned David was going away for a week. I saw David off at the airport and went to work. By 1pm I started to feel a gnawing anxiety which began to grow in size and pace. By the time I saw the GP I had a feeling of foreboding. As I told her of the events of the previous evening, I connected with my own words and the realization of what the fluid could have been began to dawn. I checked my watch. David was already in the air.

Trying to reassure me, the GP let me listen to the baby's heartbeat and that lifted me a little. She arranged my admission to hospital. I went home, saw the children in from school, left my mother in law with them and drove to the hospital. On the way I called my friend Marion and she arrived a short time after me with another friend and colleague, Julie. Within an hour I had been scanned and a kind registrar confirmed my fears. There was no amniotic fluid left.

There are no words to describe the terror I felt and I could see the fear and distress on the faces of my dear friends. I was transferred to another hospital by ambulance - a journey etched on my memory. I contacted my family and again Theresa flew over to be with me. Much later that evening I was told that there was a slim chance that the baby would make enough fluid to sustain him or herself. I would be scanned in the morning to check. The more likely outcome would be the onset of labour.

Poor David. So far away and distraught at these events. We talked intermittently throughout the night trying to comfort each other over all those miles. There would be no return flight until the morning. I paced the floor, sometimes praying, more often begging God to save my baby. I talked to my little baby pleading with her or him to hang on......

The next morning I walked through a room full of happy, heavily pregnant women to the scanner. I couldn't look. The technician was gentle. No fluid. The baby was curled up and alive. I went back to my room. Theresa went for a shower and in that space I demanded of God that he expedite the inevitable so that I didn't have to endure another night like the last.

He must have heard me that one time. By 11.30 am I was in labour. Marion unexpectedly arrived. She had felt compelled to come. Together she and Theresa carried me through. James was born at 16.50 pm. He was taken away. David arrived shortly afterwards.

I was calm. I wanted to see my baby. James Aidan Pearson. When I held him for the first time I was unprepared for the overwhelming love and serenity I felt. He was beautiful, perfect, complete, peaceful and tiny. I just loved him. He had opened a door for me. All those years of, 'Am I or aren't I a real mother?' Now I was. I thanked him. And I was fully aware that this may have been my only chance. I didn't know then that my heart had been shattered into a million pieces....... That realization came later. Much later.

I wanted to see the children before I went to theatre for minor surgery. Their pinched, pale faces made my heart ache with love for them and my darling David too. Exhausted, frightened and bewildered. I was sorry to have been the cause of such distress to them.

The next day I held James again on my own. I admired his hands, his feet, and his little nose. I talked to him, told him how long I'd waited for him and how much I loved him. I told him how desperately I had wanted him. A priest came and blessed us both. In the end, I didn't find it hard to let him go. He had already gone. Kind staff had ensured I had my footprints and photos.

I spent another 3 days in hospital. I had blood transfusions, intravenous antibiotics and tried to get stronger. I learnt that nurses are born, not made. An important lesson. I didn't want cards or flowers or visitors. I was glad however to see Angela, a friend and support at other tough times in my life and who I knew would really understand how big a blow this was for me. The days passed. The nights were long. Waking up in the mornings was agony. That lasted for weeks and months. The sound of new babies crying on the floor above my room compounded the pain. I felt empty and drained and I longed for oblivion. I began to plan a funeral for my son.

The day after my discharge from hospital we had a beautiful mass at our parish church. The sun shone. The music and singing was beautiful and we were supported by our dear friends. We brought James to the church in his little white coffin and I carried him on my lap. It felt right.

Three days later we again collected him and kept him at home overnight before embarking the next day on his final journey. I hardly slept .I didn't want to waste a precious moment of us all being together as family under the same roof. There would only be this one night when we were six and not five. The next morning in the sunshine, David and I took him by car to Ireland and in the presence of my brothers, sisters and oldest friend we laid him to rest alongside my father. That was a special day.

I can hardly believe that all this happened almost 10 months ago. The journey was just starting and I was about to enter a new world. The world of the grief stricken.

So much at the beginning was about feeling disconnected from the world. You could see and hear and make contact with others, but it was strangely muffled contact, as if there was an invisible bubble around you. Simple tasks,

126

once done instinctively, suddenly required thought, planning, and more time than ever before. Poor concentration made reading difficult and there were frequent memory lapses. Previous sources of pleasure in life felt meaningless and empty. I often felt that I was coaching myself, 'get up', 'get washed', 'show interest', 'smile' 'answer the phone', 'don't have another glass of wine' (not always successful!).

In those early months especially, the numbness was often punctuated by acute episodes of distress. These were mainly precipitated by the expected things; a return to hospital for follow up, friends having babies, pregnant women in the supermarket queue, James' due date, my niece calling her new baby son James in the days before Christmas, and often by the onset of yet another period..... After these episodes I felt like I'd been mangled in the drum of a great big machine with serrated edges. When it had finished tossing me around, it spat me out. I didn't know if I could stand or walk or feel or even recognise myself.

It's a solo journey too - an often selfish, self-obsessed and exhausting journey. Especially as it progresses. Time marches on for those around you but for you it crawls. As a consequence you fall behind.

That said, I have been hugely blessed in the people who've walked along some of the way with me and encouraged me to keep going forward. My darling husband who is patient, gentle and loyal. My children who have comforted me and forgiven my absent mind. My friends who try to encourage me to rejoin the world. My family, sisters especially. My GP. And a counsellor from the hospital, who continues to help me to pick up some of the million pieces of my heart, enables me to be brave enough to look at the damage and set about trying to put them back together.

I miss the girl who bounced out of the house that morning in March, innocent, happy and excited about motherhood. I wonder will she ever be back. The woman who walks out the same door these days is little slower, more measured, a little smaller....

But at least she is walking out of the house each day now.

She goes to work

She feeds her family

She cares for her elderly mother

She helps at the school fete

She's planning a family holiday

Because she's moving forward.....slowly...... just inches at a time.....

Quietly carrying her darling James with her.

Céline Pearson

This is really an addendum to Céline's story. I'm not really sure that I'm particularly worthy to write anything about James, as he was so much more of a reality to Céline than he was to me. I guess that's how it is for most prospective fathers – none of the sickness, the physical and hormonal changes, the carrying and the intimacy of a new life being part of you. I do remember that with my other three children, they only became a genuine reality of someone to care for, someone to help, someone to hope so many things for, someone to love, when they were actually born. For James, that reality for me never had the chance to exist; for Céline it was a day-to-day consequence of their lives as one.

All the pregnancy had been elements of worry for me: would Céline be well? How would I cope with a new baby? Would he be born well? How would the three others cope? Would Céline's relationship with her stepchildren diminish? I was buoyed through much of it by Céline's irrepressible joy and optimism and a hope that things would turn out well in the end.

It all went horribly wrong so quickly. All fine midday and looking forward to a few days away with my brother-in-law and by 6pm, a dread of what wasn't being told over the phone and the resulting turbulent sea of helplessness whipping me in alternate waves of fear and hopefulness. Honestly, my biggest fears were for Céline and not for James. Céline was my reality, my now. James was a 'to be', a future possibility like the hope that you'll get that job you always wanted, or being able to clean bowl Geoff Boycott who just happened to turn up at the local village match – something thoroughly pleasant, a sincere hope but not a reality. Céline and the children were my reality.

I got back and I had missed the birth, James hadn't been given the opportunity to become my reality, I hadn't been given the opportunity to become his. Céline seemed fine but not fine, surreally calm but detached, emotionally detached. She was in shock. Over the next days and weeks her emotional

128

maelstrom was frightening, the intensity of her grief harrowing and my ability to comfort her minimal. Not that I didn't try and not that I was a stranger to grief – my first wife died young when the kids were 4, 2 and six months and I really felt that I had known grief. Perhaps I hadn't, or perhaps I'd just been so caught up in three tiny lives that I had to somehow lift beyond it, that I had no time for it. Her emotion was just so shockingly raw, so dispiritingly raw. I did all the things that I could, the kids were fantastic and also did all that they could but we were in a parallel existence, Céline was there but not with us; she was simply with James, yet James was not with any of us.

The services and funeral had to be organised. Organised they were (some small contribution to alleviate Céline's distress that I felt that I actually could do) and they were lovely. They were also stressful, the need to put on the "I'm sure we'll get over it" face to all but not being sure you will. I hoped, no more than a hope – more a soulful prayer, that a small dead body in the ground would somehow mark a turning point, a walking away, a moving on, a return to life as we knew it.

And so it has gone on; more soulful prayers than I can count for a return to life as we knew it. Not just for me but for our family, for the five people who together represent a core of mutual love that has carried us through much in fifteen years. It could so easily have been six people in that core but that was a sincere hope, not to be a reality.

It does get easier; time is a healer but not all wounds heal without leaving scars and sometimes impairment. For me, more detached from James because I wasn't the carrier, and much more aware that "you are where you are, not where you wish you were", I just want everything back to where it was. For Céline, she just wants James; she understands the logic of where we are but it's more difficult to accept. Perhaps accepting it somehow makes it look or feel as if you didn't really care; denying the depth of your loss makes the loss feel less important and so a betrayal. Perhaps it's a Venus thing –focussed on the "if only" more than the "now, what next".

It does get easier but it's never clear if it's genuinely easier rather than just better hidden. The only thing I believe that you can do is to look back and measure what it's like now against what it was like 6 weeks ago or 6 months ago, trying to be objective rather than naively hopeful about "it's getting better", and I do believe that it is.

As I said this is more an addendum to Céline's story and I feel a little fraudulent writing it; hers is much more a Farewell to James, mine more a heartfelt farewell to the hopes that I would have had for James had he lived.

We move forward. Forward, because that's the only direction I feel prepared to accept for this core of five, a core of five that should have been six.

David Pearson

There is little of what is past but memories.
Memories are links to the past from the present.
The past fades.
It will always have value but its essence lies in helping us to understand
what we have had and where we have come from.
Its highest value comes in using it to chart our future.

We must embrace the future.
Within it lies risk, but within it lies opportunity.
We must greet it warmly and not be fearful of the changes it brings.

Fear is but an excuse to live in the past.
It comes in many guises – indecision, uncertainty, trepidation, procrastination, even as despair and anguish
But it is fear.

Faith in ourselves, our future, our worth, allows us to conquer fear.
It encourages us to grasp opportunity and improve our lot.
Faith helps us to realize that the future is friendly even though the past may have been harsh.

Without faith to risk, life is flat.
It has no peaks of pleasure, only troughs of despair.
Pleasure can only truly be appreciated against the contrast of despair.
Faith helps us to tilt the balance of life so that we may leave behind us a legacy of pleasure for ourselves and our children,
And despair can then itself become a memory in the past.

David Pearson

To Kester

*You, child, who were born into my golden hope
But softly died into my grey despair,
Who, though never seen or heard or felt,
Dwell in love forever present where
Sweet beginnings cluster round my long lost dreams,
And happy memories of what could never be,
Cocooned in amber, glowing warm and bright,
From pain of loss have grown 'til I can see
You, child, retain your presence in my life
More powerfully than anyone foresaw
Because your life, though brief, has touched my soul;
You are my much-loved son for evermore.*

*You, child, who wove dark sorrow round my heart
And cast me far into a foreign land
Now dwell in sweet contentment safe within
Soft memories forever close at hand.*

*You, child, who walk within me sight unseen,
Whose face returns to light my fantasies,
Whose name is graven smiling on my dreams,
Your being is forever part of me.*

Sue Young

131

Ned Stanley
Rufus Pennant

6 November 2002 –
12 July 2003

Ned

We found Ned dead in his cot after coming home from the
school summer ball. That moment changed our lives forever.
Four years later, writing this, I am shaking, nervous – such is
the impact of the deep shock and sadness from the tragedy
of losing one's child.

It was a Saturday. For once we were all home, all day. All six of us, with four
children aged 7 and under; a very happy and loving family, close knit,
chaotic, carefree and fun. It was hot. It was the summer of 2003. Ironically,
Don had spent some of the day inside putting up a new bed for Maisie, our
number 3. It was high time Ned went into a cot and Maisie moved on into
a bed.

What a waste of time that was. It was Ned's first night in a cot. And his last
on earth. We threw the cot away.

No one yet knows for certain why cot death occurs – and it is still too painful
for me to study the theories around. We travelled to hospital by ambulance,
the nurses still working with Ned to revive him. It was at this point that the
word Hope took on new depths. We had found him at home possibly several
hours after he had passed away. I had picked him up and whilst on the phone
to the ambulance, he was sick. I had massive hope he had choked and was
coming round. Later I learned this was his stomach closing and a signal of the
final end. In the ambulance and at the hospital, whilst they were working on
him, we hoped he would be OK. Even by that stage however, if he had
survived, he would have been brain damaged – but you still hope.

132

I suppose it is that knowing that crashes you into your new life. The feeling the world has let you down, the loss of trust in everyday life; the knowing that you are going to change as a person. It's frightening and scary. It tears relationships apart.

Of course you need to know why. Why? Why? The nagging question is a constant. I even got myself into thinking it was because Ned rhymed with dead. If he was called Clive, would he still be alive? I realised I was never going to understand why it happened to him, our beautiful boy with his broad grin, happy disposition and much loved number 4. I had to settle with the fact that he had loved life, all of it. He had never had Calpol. At 8 months he was fully integrated within the family and local community. He was beginning to furniture walk. Invincible. Our life was a cocoon of sunny days and freedom. We were complete, naive and wanting it that way.

At 37, I had never seen, let alone held, a dead body. Yet Jemima, just 7, wanted to come and say goodbye in the chapel at Wycombe General. I will never forget the way she fell to her knees, pleading, yet realising he was gone. Her little brother.

Shock seems to make one's body go into overdrive – this kind of focus, not my control, but an out of body control envelops you. My main focus was to ensure the rest of the family were ok. If I fell apart, what would happen to them? I couldn't let myself. I made sure they were still in the right place at the right time, that they had food on the table, had stories at bedtime. We needed their lives to stay as normal as possible. My time came later, almost exactly two years – we had moved house, built a house and had had another boy. I realised I was shattered, completely exhausted. But I am lucky; I haven't collapsed or been depressed.

The impact of his death on our family, friends and within the local community has been huge. We have always been very open about Ned. We have made sure his name is still alive at home, we have a star for him in the sky, and his stocking still appears at Christmas. The children need it. This is one way in which Don and I, as parents, have helped our other children deal with their loss. He is buried close to where we live and where the children are at school, so we can visit him as often as we wish. I really believe this has been the focal point of us being able to accept what has happened. Children need to express themselves and by being very open, they can question, comment and include whenever they need to. Even now I hear them talk to friends in the car –

133

"that's Ned's", or "did you know Ned didn't like such and such?" Even Leo, our blessed number 5 who never met Ned, saves things for him, blows kisses to the stars. It works for us. Dandelion seeds that float in the sky are called Neddy's; tiny conkers are put on his grave; when all goes quiet at home we say 'Ned overhead'. We all feel he is around us watching, laughing and guiding.

And yes, Don and I have changed as people, of course we have. But time has helped us accept that change. We can't get rid of it; we have to work with it. Four years later, life is easier. I have some spare brain space for other thoughts. But the pain still grabs my inner heart; I still feel it ache when I think of him. I cope by feeling him around me all the time; he's my shadow, and I almost ask his approval before doing anything. Several times people referred to Ned as an angel. He looked angelic; he behaved angelically. Maybe he was an angel, called back to heaven. I find that hard to accept. Why weren't we told he was only to be here a short time? How could anyone be so cruel as to take your child away? I like to think he was so happy in his dreams he forgot to wake up. Or maybe he never wanted to grow up – our very own Peter Pan.

We have written the following on his gravestone. We saw it on a bench overlooking the river shortly before he died:

Remembering you is easy, we do every day
But missing you is heartache, which never goes away

To you, Ned, you are forever in our hearts and constantly in our thoughts. We love you.

Allie Pennant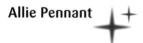

Just over 8 months old when he died, I constantly reflect on how amazing Ned was at the tender age of 8 months.

At the time we had three other children, aged 7, 5 and 2¾, all who had gone through the same stage, developed and grown, as we all have done. Cot death happens to others, not to us, and anyway surely he was past the age for cot death. No!!

What struck me greatly at the time was how close parents are to their children. How well they know their characteristics, their patterns, their loves, their hates and their needs in ways that no-one else such as grandparents, godparents or even very close friends do.

The frustration was that we knew how fantastic he was, what a special child he was, but no-one else really had the opportunity to see that and to really get to know him. Ned was really an angel.

To soften the excruciating blow of his death I often conclude that we had only borrowed Ned from God and that he was such a wonderful boy, an angel, God had taken him back to heaven to entertain all those others who had died. Ned was always laughing.

It is impossible to transfer ones own memories and feelings to others for them to see and feel the same. This can be expressed in words but this is not sufficient to allow others to understand what we had lost. I knew that people were feeling really sorry for our family rather than because Ned, as a person, wasn't around any more. I wanted the sympathy to be because he had gone, not because we had lost someone.

Above is the epitaph from his gravestone. For me much of the missing lies in the expectation of his development; his young fun years of learning to walk and to talk; the school years of sports days, concerts and pantomimes; the post school growth into adulthood and independence and then hopefully marriage and children.

We can only imagine this. We are however very lucky to be able to experience this through our other children. Others may not be so lucky and I feel for them.

Even though Ned was only 8 months old when he slipped away he has had a profound effect on us. He seemed to be way beyond his years and have an unusual understanding of us and his surroundings – an angel, we miss you.

Don Pennant

135

The following is a poem put through our door anonymously the day after he died. We each have a laminated copy, with a photo of him on the other side, which is credit card size and lives in our wallets. Someone very insightful wrote it for us and we have found it very comforting.

Ned

Mummy do not weep for me for I am fine
Tell Daddy not to fret
I am only sleeping till we meet again
Thank my sisters for taking such good care of me
and my brother for making me smile
You gave me life Mummy
You kept me safe from harm and surrounded me with love
Do not regret anything Mummy
Let it be
Nothing or nobody can change our destiny
I will always be with you Mummy
A pretty flower
Birdsong or children's laughter
But mostly you will feel me in your heart
and see me in the faces of my sisters and brother
Mummy do not weep for me for I am fine

Anon

136

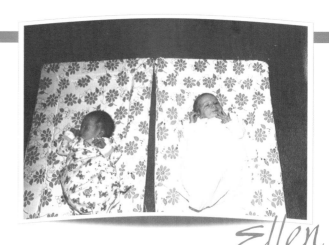

Ellen Ruth Poll

13 January 1979 –
2 February 1979

Ellen

Howard and I were desperately excited when, at 20 weeks, I found out that we were having twins – we couldn't wait to introduce them to our daughter, Louise, who was two years old.

I had pre-eclampsia, and was induced at 37 weeks. 24 hours later, on 13th January, I had an emergency caesarean due to foetal and maternal distress. My little girl Ellen was born first, although she wouldn't have been first if the twins had been delivered naturally. She was born at 10.27am weighing 6lb 9oz, and Sam followed at 10.29am weighing 6lb 8oz.

In the days after their birth I was very ill due to the pre-eclampsia and blood loss. The babies were taken to special care because I was so unwell. I spent about a week in hospital and during that time actually said to Howard, "I'll never wheel the twin pram out" thinking it was me who wouldn't make it rather than one of the babies.

I remember my concern at the time was mainly for our daughter, Lou, and how she would feel about not one but two new babies in the family. She was fantastic though, and from the time I came home it was obvious that she was going to be brilliant – she was mummy's little helper. I was very aware that she had to be included and that was my priority. For that period it felt very important that it was just the five of us.

In the three weeks that I got to know Ellen it was clear that she was very much more dominant than Sam. I breastfed both the twins but Ellen was greedy and we used to call her 'Miss Piggy' as she would take all the cream of my milk and leave Sam with the watered down milk! At the time a midwife gave me

137

some very bad advice; I had extreme calcium deficiency and Ellen was taking a lot of the good stuff, so she advised me to breastfeed Ellen and bottle feed Sam. Due to this, I became very unwell and Lou was sent to stay with her Nanna, Howard's mum. As it turned out she went there five days before Ellen died, so she wasn't at home when it happened which I am pleased about.

On the morning Ellen died, I fed her at around 4am. I then fed Sam at around 5am and put him down at 6am. I checked Ellen as I always did and she was alive then. She was due to have her next feed an hour later at 7am, but didn't wake. When the phone woke us at 8.15am, I asked Howard to check the babies. Although Ellen hadn't woken, there was no sense of dread at all; we were just pleased to have had some extra sleep. But when Howard came back, he walked around the side of the bed and just said "Ellen's dead".

It was a nightmare. I was only 26 and had been so happy and had no idea what to do. I telephoned the doctor and asked what I should do. They said the doctor would come immediately – it didn't even cross my mind to call an ambulance, I was so stunned. I actually don't know what we did between that phone call and the doctor arriving – it must have been at least 10 minutes. I heard the doctor's car and as he ran up the stairs I remember shouting, "Please tell me she's not dead". By the time the doctor came, Howard had fetched Sam from his crib – I couldn't have gone into their room – and I just held on to him so tightly as though I could never let him go again. The doctor was almost as distressed as us; he had never had anything like this happen to him. I remember that he came and sat on our bed and just held my hand; he was as good as he could have been given the fact that he had had no experience or training in how to deal with situations such as this.

My mother had come as soon as I had phoned her and acted as if nothing had happened, which was her way of coping. I remember her saying, "Isn't it a lovely day. Shall I draw the curtains?" The midwife arrived to do her daily visit and was obviously greeted with this terrible situation. She, too, had no idea what to say or do; by the time she arrived I was sitting downstairs clinging onto Sam and wouldn't let anyone take him from me. He was due a feed and I asked the midwife if I should now breast feed him – I had no confidence – she said she thought it was better that I continued to bottle feed him – such unhelpful advice and something I regret. Although my mother was adamant that I shouldn't see Ellen, which I know was well-intentioned because she wanted to protect me, I overruled her and the midwife took me up to see

138

her. She looked awful, and sadly that is the last memory I have of her. I had only a matter of minutes with Ellen and it is my hugest regret that I didn't spend more time with her.

We decided that we wanted to go and get Lou from Howard's parents. I remember spending the whole 30-minute car journey with my hand on Sam's chest to make sure that he was breathing. When we arrived at Howard's mother's house, Lou kept asking "Where's the other baby?" but Howard didn't want to tell her in front of his mother. He wanted to wait until we were by ourselves. When I asked him why, he said, "If I say her name I will never stop crying." Howard and I have always handled our grief very differently.

When we got back my mother said to me, "Do you want to know when the funeral is?" It was very low key, no-one wore black at my request but I don't remember much, except that Lou came down with whooping cough on the day. The next few weeks were stressful because Lou was very poorly. The doctor wanted her to be admitted to hospital but I didn't want her out of my sight; I wanted the family to be together. We just got through that and then when Sam was six weeks old – three weeks after Ellen's death – he was diagnosed with a heart murmur and the doctor who saw him was extremely unsympathetic. Ellen's notes were still strapped to Sam's, which was heartbreaking in itself. It turned out to be innocent thank goodness, but it gave me lots more to worry about!!

I have huge regrets about not making the funeral arrangements myself. My mum did ask what I wanted Ellen to wear and I gave her a little nightie, but apart from that I didn't have much to do with it and so wish that I had. This in particular has had a huge impact on me and when my father died, I did everything I wished I had done for Ellen. I was with him when he died; I spent time with him after his death; I left classical music playing when there was no-one with him; I dressed him in what he would have wanted to wear and often went to see him in the undertakers.

In Ellen's case, my mother had thought it best that I shouldn't go and see her at the undertakers. If, God forbid, one of my children lost a baby or child I would make sure that they made the decision themselves, and would help and support them to make those decisions. You have to go through it; otherwise I believe it makes the grief worse. In my case it wasn't until 16 years later – when I discovered CBC and did my first fundraising ball – that I felt I understood my reactions and in some way came to terms with Ellen's death.

I realised that I should have stood up for myself and made my own decisions. If CBC had been around when Ellen died, I would have had a very different experience and all the health professionals concerned would have been better equipped to deal with the situation. However, I am a positive person and do believe that life has to go on. You can't let the experience consume you – especially when you have two small children to look after.

I went on to have another daughter, Lorna, after Ellen's death. Funnily enough I was never as fearful around her as I was with Sam. When I was expecting Lorna I was convinced that she had a cleft palate. I desperately wanted a normal delivery but she was a transverse lie, and again I was given bad advice to have a general anaesthetic; but when I came round, there she was and she was perfect. I had been worried in case she looked like Ellen. In fact, she was the spitting image but it didn't matter at all. From the age of 6 weeks she slept from 6pm until 8am. I was much more chilled out with Lorna, whereas I was always far more fearful with Sam.

All three of my children have been affected by Ellen. She has left a fantastic legacy, as they are all very special. I really believe it is thanks to her that they are so intuitive and we are such a close family.

Jill Poll

I remember waking up on that day. I went into the back bedroom and tried to wake Ellen first, she was face down in the moses basket. I picked her up and turned her over, but it was clear that she was dead. I made sure Sam was ok, then went to tell Jill about Ellen. I didn't want Jill to see her. We sat and cuddled Sam. Emotionally, as a Dad, it was terrible; I felt shocked, empty, and didn't know how to cope with the situation apart from doing all the practical stuff. It was a bit of a blur really.

As a family it drew us closer together. On Sam's birthday I have mixed feelings, and I am more reminded by Jill than anything else.

It took a long time for me to grieve; I shut it away and just went to work the very next day. I was probably not as supportive of Jill at that time as I should have been, but it is the way I have coped. I don't dwell on it as much as Jill.

Howard Poll

I was nearly 3 years old when my little sister Ellen died. I don't have a specific memory of finding out that she had died (perhaps because I was staying with my Nanna at the time), and sadly I don't have any memories of having Ellen in my life. I love that we have some photographs of me with the twins, and mum often tells me that I was very helpful in those precious few weeks of Ellen's life. Apparently I used to get up during the night to help her change nappies and feed – maybe I was destined to be a midwife even then! I can't remember mum and dad telling me that Ellen had died - it was just something that was such a huge part of our everyday life.

The years after Ellen's death were very difficult for mum and dad, but mum would always vocalise her grief more – usually on Sam's birthday, at Christmas time or at other important family occasions. I guess we all felt that there was always someone missing. I think dad has found it much more difficult to talk about Ellen dying and has always dealt with his grief in a much more private way. Sam is just an amazing young chap, I am immensely proud of him and all that he is. I find it very sad, as I'm sure that losing a twin is a very difficult experience. I know that he thinks about her on a daily basis and often wonders whether it should have been him. Despite living with these feelings he is an incredible young man.

I often wonder whether I chose to become a midwife as a direct result of Ellen's death. It is certainly true that I am very passionate about my job and thrive to support families through the childbearing process with minimal stress and upheaval. It has been very difficult at times when I have had to help a family to deal with their own loss. I would like to think that I'm more understanding and supportive in these circumstances, I certainly feel I can empathise with these desperately sad situations as a direct result of our experiences as a family.

As a whole, Ellen's short but very precious life has had an incredibly powerful effect on all of us. None of us would be the people we are today if it hadn't been for her. I miss her a lot and often spend time daydreaming about her...

Louise Poll

When I was old enough to truly understand what had happened to Ellen, it saddened me greatly and looking back I do think it made me more of a sensitive and inquisitive child. I'm still not sure of why it happened to Ellen and not me, and it still feels today as if part of me is missing. As I have grown older, I have wanted to understand more and as a result I'm keen to follow in my Mum's footsteps in terms of helping others who have suffered the same unfortunate grief.

I am sure that the experience my parents had, how they dealt with that and how they have since brought us up has made me more of a sensitive person than I perhaps would have been, but this is a legacy of Ellen's which I am proud to associate myself with. I still feel Ellen's presence and talking to her sometimes helps in times of difficulty; it has an extremely calming effect. For example, a few years ago my Dad had a serious car accident, which he luckily got out of unscathed, and I still like to think she was perhaps looking after him that day, like she does all of us.

As we were twins, our birthday can obviously sometimes be a difficult and emotional time for my parents, but that's something I'd never want hidden from me. In a way it keeps Ellen's memory alive, and that's very important to me, and especially to my Mum and Dad.

When I visit Ellen's grave at Barham, it really hits home how much we lost as a family, but also how much I lost as a twin. I love to think about how she would look, if she'd have a daft sense of humour like the rest of us, and how she'd have loved to travel the world like me, and all such things. It helps me deal with the thought that I lost someone who would have been so very special to me, as Louise and Lorna are now.

It's very emotional for us all when we visit Barham, but it's also a very special time to think about her. What I love most is that it's a place of immense beauty and peace, and if anything it brings us closer together as a family knowing she's resting there with other members of our family who also meant so much to us. It's both wonderful and important that we can be open about our feelings, and although Dad tends to keep his feelings to himself to a degree, each person deals with grief differently and I utterly respect that.

Considering Ellen's short time with us, her legacy is remarkable. She is never out of our thoughts for long and I am confident that as a result of what we went through as a family all those years ago, we have become an extremely tight and supportive unit.

Ellen's legacy has also encouraged us as a family to become involved in Charity events and fundraising in her memory. I for one hope to do more in the future, and only have to look as far as my Mum and the other hardworking fundraisers at CBC for inspiration.

On a personal note, I still think now that it could so easily have been me that was taken away too soon. And so I try to think of how good a person Ellen would have been, the lust for life she would have had, the places she would have liked to see and experience, and the ambition and sheer energy she would have carried into her professional and personal life – and as a result that only makes me want to achieve and experience more myself – I guess, in a way, it encourages me to live my life for her too.

Sam Poll

I can never single out a time as to when I found out about Ellen's death; I've just grown up knowing that I would have had a sister, but sadly she died as a baby.

It's not until I had grown up that I really thought about the impact of losing Ellen on my parents and in turn on Sam and Lou. Initially I felt slightly removed from the grieving process, as I wasn't alive when she was born, and also had a feeling that she should be here, as planned, and not me. However, mum always reassured me that she wanted four children regardless.

I do feel that there is a massive hole in our family without Ellen present and it makes me feel incredibly sad when I think of what our family would be like now if she were to have lived, the dynamics of the sibling relationships and the family as a whole. Although all three of us are close, Sam and I are only two years apart and share the same social circle and friends, which is so important to me. Our birthdays are also only a day apart. I love the fact we are so close, but I feel for him that he doesn't have his twin here to share a close relationship with.

As a family we have always talked a great deal about Ellen, more so since Mum found the CBC and I think it's an incredibly important process to go through when you have lost a loved one. I understand that it's never been easy for my dad to talk about losing Ellen and I believe it's his right to not want to share his feelings like we do, as much as it is our right to want to share ours more freely.

143

I have a great sense of happiness knowing that we are so involved with CBC, as I feel this keeps Ellen's legacy going. She will always have this within our family, but having the Ball makes it all that more special to celebrate the time my family had with her. I have a great yearning to have known her and I feel heartbroken that I didn't, but I do know a wonderful memory of her lives on through the amazing work that we are involved with.

Lorna Poll

Just Those Few Weeks

For those few weeks -
I had you to myself.
And that seems too short a time
To be changed so profoundly.

In those few weeks -
I came to know you....
And to love you.
You came to trust me with your life.
Oh, what a life I had planned for you!

Just those few weeks -
When I lost you,
I lost a lifetime of hopes, plans, dreams, and aspirations...
A slice of my future simply vanished overnight.

Just those few weeks -
It wasn't enough to convince others
How special and important you were.
How odd, a truly unique person has recently died
And no one is mourning the passing.

Just a mere few weeks -
And no 'normal' person would cry all night
Over a tiny, unfinished baby,
Or get depressed and withdraw day after endless day.
No one would, so why am I?

You were just those few weeks my little one
You darted in and out of my life too quickly
But it seems that's all the time you needed
To make my life so much richer-
And give me a small glimpse of eternity.   ***Susan Erlin***

144

Thomas Joseph Rodin

21 April 1995 – 11 January 2001

Thomas

Thomas was amazing; big, handsome, kind and clever. Andrea and I adored him as did his older brother Ben and his little sister Hannah. Everyone who met him loved him. He was warm and giving and had a smile that was reflected in every face it met.

He was just three months short of his sixth birthday when it happened. It was almost as if he just woke up and died. At 6am it was such a normal day. I was in the bathroom, the first up as always on a work day. Thomas' bedroom was right next door and when he began to cry I heard him immediately. It was 6.20 a.m. He said he had a headache so I brought him into the bathroom and gave him some Calpol. Andrea joined us, woken by his crying. By 6.25 Thomas could hardly speak and by 6.30 he was unconscious. Andrea knew it was serious but I thought that he was just asleep. Urged on by her concern I rushed him to the hospital.

It took no more than ten minutes to get him there. I can still feel the limp weight of his body in my arms as I carried him from the car into A&E and over to the administrator's desk. They took my details and made us wait. After about 20 minutes we were seen by the triage nurse. She examined Thomas who hardly stirred. Then she sent us back to the waiting area. It was only when Thomas wet himself that I demanded urgent help. They took us through to a cubicle and made us wait... hours. Thomas was heavy but all that time

145

I kept him cradled on my lap. Several times I got up with him in my arms and looked outside for some help, but there was nobody there.

Thank God for that nurse who eventually passed the open door of our cubicle.

"Is everything alright?"

"No, my son needs help."

What a change; doctors and nurses, from one to twenty in less than five seconds. But it was too late. In truth it was too late at 6.20 that morning, the moment that Thomas woke up. He had a massive bleed in his brain from a ruptured cerebral aneurism. I remember the X ray that we were shown, just a mass of white, the photographic colour of his blood. 'Odds of one in fifteen million for a child of his age,' we were later told by the consultant that operated on him. Not long enough.

Thomas was moved from our local hospital to the John Radcliffe in Oxford for the last day and a half of his unconscious life. The staff there were remarkable but even their skills couldn't bring him back. Nothing could. He was pronounced dead on the afternoon of January 11th 2001 and at just gone midnight, Andrea and I walked away from our darling son shortly before his body was operated on for organ donation. Who knows exactly how much of us was left there with him.

How do you describe a world that has lost its sunlight? A series of vague, blurred images merged into each other. I do remember one particular experience though, very soon after Thomas died. I was standing in the kitchen gazing aimlessly out of the window. I could sense the earth under my feet. It was moving very slowly and taking me in a direction that I didn't want to go... away from Thomas and his life. It was a feeling of despairing helplessness crushing my deepest desire to be a father who protected his children from serious harm.

Ben was then 8 and Hannah 2. Our family of four now had to succeed on a journey of life which had begun with a nightmare of death. The social worker at the John Radcliffe told us that other bereaved parents had said that their experience of those first years was like standing with your back to the sea and never knowing when the next big wave was going to hit you. I think that's a good analogy.

It is now almost seven years since the start of that journey. The fact that we have got as far as we have is nothing to do with a clichéd strength or bravery, however appealingly simple that might seem. For us it has been a complex combination of love, humour, resilience and many other qualities that make human beings so special. Nor is our family four; the space in the middle of the back seat of the car might be empty but each of us carries a part of Thomas with us. Hannah, who is now nearly 9, speaks often of Thomas and keeps a photo of the two of them by her bedside so that she can look at it as she drifts off to sleep. Ben, who is 15, talks less frequently of his 'Buddy Brother' as the two of them used to call each other. But his love for Thomas is more than obvious to anyone willing to look beneath the surface and his bedroom also has photos of the two of them together. Seeing Ben and Hannah grow and develop has produced rich green shoots of life for their parents in a ground which not very long ago seemed to be made of nothing but rock and stone.

Thomas' headstone is decorated with 'Thomas Island', a representation of the beautiful floral creation sent by his primary school on the day of the funeral. It has palm trees and a hut with Thomas' favourite beanie babies scattered amongst them. At the base of the headstone is a poem by Ben Jonson, which captures the essence of Thomas' short life.

It is not growing like a tree
In bulk, doth make man better be,
Or standing long an oak, three hundred year,
To fall a log at last, dry, bald and sere:
A lily of a day
Is fairer far in May
Although it fall and die that night,
It was the plant and flower of light.
In small proportions we just beauties see;
And in short measures life may perfect be.

Ben Jonson 1572 - 1637

Peter Rodin

147

Adelina
Scott Lin

10 October 1986 – 27 July 2005

Adelina

My favourite description of Adelina – an 'irresistible rogue' – came from one of her school reports. Adelina was as irrepressible as she was irresistible, a very ebullient, lively and witty girl who never bothered to hand in her homework or get herself organised, except when it really mattered to her. She was clever, but wore her cleverness lightly. She was shy, but not with friends and family, with whom her keen sense of mischief always prevailed.

Her friends looked to her for laughs, and her sense of fun was evidently contagious. She fancied herself as a 'mad scientist' and thought of studying Chemistry, but she was also a gifted linguist who loved the arts and after a year of deliberation had finally opted to study Classics at university. One of her ambitions was to fund a course which would combine Chemistry with Classics – it was typical of her to straddle divides and then seek to build bridges for others.

Adelina was remarkably quick on the uptake. She'd ponder a Sudoku for a few minutes, and then fill it in all in one go. She had an exceptionally good memory and the kind of intelligence that could cut corners – something I greatly admired. Teachers and school friends would be exasperated by her grades which were excellent without any evidence of work. Once at prep school she was called up to read her essay. Since she hadn't written it, but didn't want to be found out, she took out some random paper and pretended to read the first page and a bit. The teacher, smelling a rat, asked her to go back to the beginning and read it again. She calmly set to! I loved both her chutzpah and her ability. There was a disarming conflict for the observer, though apparently not for Adelina, between her shyness and audacity, her sense of natural modesty and conviction that nothing was impossible.

The fact that Adelina was such fun, such good company, and such a 'deserving' person is a great consolation to me. One might think it would make me more miserable at her premature death, at the apparent injustice of her loss. She had so much to live for, and she had such a joie de vivre, why should she have been denied the chance of a long and fulfilling life? But such questions are pointless or worse – they encourage despair. Since there is no justice in accidental death, and since there is no bringing her back, I remind myself that such things 'just happen' and that one can either despair and die, persevere with stoicism – or, better still, grow with love and gratitude for what one has been given, not just regret and resentment at what has been taken.

I tend to find consolation in the fact that Adelina lived her short span to the full. As a friend of hers said to me, she packed more lives into her two decades than most people would in seven. Her whole philosophy was based on carpe diem and her call to make the most of life, which she so joyfully did, is one of her enduring legacies. Several people have told me that after reading Adelina's story, which includes some of her journal entries from her last trip, in the collection of poems that I published (Adelina, Birsay Publishers, 2007), they have changed their own attitude to life and decided to engage with the choices available to them more pro-actively. It's a great source of consolation to know that Adelina's love of life remains a force for the good.

Adelina had gone off inter-railing and I was driving to Scotland on my way to Orkney with my mother who has Alzheimer's. I remember having nightmares about torrents and floods and water the night Adelina died. When I awoke and saw that it was a nice day, I felt both relieved and lifted by the sunshine. We picked my brother up from the airport and continued our drive north. Barely out of Glasgow he received a phone call from a friend in Zermatt, where we have a flat, and asked me to stop the car so that he could talk with him privately. Clearly, something had happened to someone, but when he got back in the car he asked me to drive on and as we were approaching a toll bridge, I figured it wasn't anything that would require us to turn back.

149

However, when he received a second call, also from Zermatt, I knew this concerned Adelina. I tried to call her, couldn't get through. Called my son Anton to ask him if he had her travel companion's number. "Have you spoken to Baba" (Daddy), he asked? "No". "You should call him Mummy". I called my ex-husband. Time had stopped. My senses were all on the alert. Everything was amplified.

When I reached my ex on the phone, he was in hysterics. He shouted "Are you sitting down? Are you sitting down?" and I knew that the worst had happened. "How? How did it happen?" He started screaming "She's dead! She's dead!" She had drowned in the river. I hung up and screamed – a primordial scream. I remember my mother putting her hand on my shoulder – I was grateful that she was reaching out to me. That small human contact mattered. My brother hadn't said a word. He didn't touch me. He suggested I move into the passenger seat and he take over the driving. We went back to Glasgow airport.

The trip to Geneva was fraught for me. My brother had booked us onto a flight via Luton, but as I didn't have my passport on me, I wasn't allowed on the Geneva flight. Anton and his father were flying from Heathrow and had my passport with them, so I took a taxi and sat in endless traffic jams hoping against hope that I would make it to Heathrow in time. The taxi driver did her best, and I was deeply grateful to her. I arrived as the flight was meant to be taking off, but by some good fortune it had been delayed so I was rushed on board at the eleventh hour. I cried silently but copiously, no sobs, no shakes, just a steady flow of tears into my cupped hands. The air hostess was kind – kept supplying me with tissues, offering a sympathetic touch. I was once again grateful for the contact, for the comfort of strangers.

We have always holidayed in Zermatt and Adelina had a tradition of dipping her feet in the river to say farewell to the place before departure. She was a water baby – always drawn to water and a very strong swimmer. She had decided to dip her toes two nights before she died but had been stopped by the police who warned her that it was dangerous. In our last conversation together, just a few hours before she died, she was full of happy chatter about what she was up to and what her plans for Italy were the next day. Italian train strikes had forced them back to Zermatt for that one night. She told me about being cautioned, about how strict the police were and what a bore it all was. I didn't think to warn her against any disobedience, to emphasise the danger.

150

Standing up in indignation against authority was part of her emerging moral identity. Would it have made a difference? It's hard not to fantasise about the small details that might have made a big difference to the final outcome. It's also hard not to feel responsible – after all, one has failed in one's ultimate responsibility as a parent: to ensure the wellbeing and survival of one's offspring. That hits hard, no matter what the circumstances.

That evening she went out again in the village. Her friend stayed at home to sleep. After midnight a young Irish Canadian, Brendan Killoran, who was working in Zermatt, walked with her to the river that runs through the middle of the village. She must have tried to dip her feet in again. Her shoes, money and passport were left neatly on a ledge under the main bridge. Brendan's coat was found thrown aside some twenty metres further down. It seems that Adelina slipped, and he jumped in to her rescue. Both of them were seen by several witnesses, close together in the water, screaming for help as they were swept under one bridge after another. His body was found in the valley where the torrent becomes a broad river. Adelina was wedged behind a rock and was harder to find and airlift from the narrow gully. Both were badly bruised and battered. I remain in awe at Brendan's act of chivalry.

The police took us to the place where Adelina had fallen in, and to where she had been found. Then to the chapel where her body was lying so that we could identify her. Cyril and Anton flew back that same day. I walked up and down the river distraught, trying to understand my daughter's last moments. Imagining her fear and suffering.

A close friend, who used to be the children's au pair, dropped everything to come and be with me. We placed flowers for Adelina and Brendan. We sat at the spot where she had fallen in.

I asked to go back to the chapel and see Adelina's body alone, and returned again during the next two days. I still don't understand any of the emotions I had on being with the body of my dead daughter. They were very strong – strong yet calm. The sense of 'at-peace' which I felt while I was with her had a transcendent quality about it. I remember how important it was to express my love for her, to assure her that everybody was full of love for her, despite our terrible sorrow and loss. And I remember that the feeling of love and peace was palpable, it hummed and filled the air in that chapel of rest where I sat, my hand on hers, unable to assimilate the feel of her cold clammy skin.

Initially she looked exactly herself, except for the bruises, a gashed lip and smashed front teeth. I was tempted to undress her. But I decided (and it was a painful and somehow counter-instinctive decision) not to, because she had always been so modest and probably wouldn't have wanted to be seen naked. I also decided not to carry on sitting next to her as she started to decompose. She was such a beautiful girl, I felt I was denying her dignity by watching her face fall away from its living semblance – again, she wouldn't have liked it. Instead I returned daily and sat outside the chapel. Near her I was at peace, next to the torrent I was in torment.

My concern that Adelina should be remembered with love made me anxious about the reaction of Brendan's friends and family. Would they hold Adelina responsible for his death? I went to speak to his friends where he worked, and later made contact with his Uncle and Aunt with whom I remain in correspondence. His mother hasn't wanted to be in touch. Her husband had also died of accidental drowning. Brendan's death leaves me deeply troubled. His self-sacrifice moves me beyond words.

Once Adelina's body had been repatriated and I was back in England there were the details of the funeral to attend to. At the funeral parlour, in the church and on other occasions, Cyril's wife would burst into tears, and his extended family, who were usually there with us, would rally round to console her. I felt like the odd man out, marginalized and disturbingly upstaged by these shows of emotion. Cyril too was much more demonstrative in his grief than I ever was – in public at least.

It's not out of principle that I don't cry in company, but because the presence of others puts me in a different gear, one in which I put my best foot forward and attend to the needs of the other rather than myself. Addressing my own concerns is something for which I need privacy. Perhaps my many years as a single mother have taught me to be a coper? Anton is much more like me in his grief. In fact he fell out with his father over this as Cyril assumed that where there was no evidence of grieving there was no grief.

In contrast, Anton and I, even in those very early days, had some very helpful exchanges – and laughs – together. We had one extended repartee over the phone from Zermatt involving all the water expressions we could think of (water under the bridge, a sinking feeling, out of one's depth etc...). At the funeral, Cyril wrote a speech which he asked Anton to read out, and which

152

Anton prefaced with a joke I greatly appreciated (he introduced himself as his 'Mum's new favourite'). Similarly, when I stood up to eulogise Adelina, which I decided to do without notes in honour of her own nascent gift at public speaking, my primary objective was to bring the congregation round from tears to laughter. Hearing the church laugh remains my proudest achievement in Adelina's memory.

I often go to the cemetery to place flowers and light candles for Adelina. Cyril has had a beautiful gravestone erected, and we sometimes bump into each other there. We did so by chance rather than design today, on her 21st birthday, and it was a delight to see her grave decked out with food, lights, flowers and balloons, surrounded by family, cousins, aunts and uncles. Adelina had always wanted the two families to be close even after the divorce, and sure enough, Cyril's family has been very generous in including me and my mother at Christmas and birthday celebrations.

My own friends have also been very good to me. The warmth and spontaneity of their embrace when they first gathered at Adelina's wake is something that changed my outlook and confirmed me in my belief that people matter infinitely more than possessions, success or any other worldly conceits. Many of my friends were either very fond of Adelina and are coping with their own sense of loss, and reminder of mortality, or they are coming to grips by proxy with that most haunting of all fears – the death of one's child.

I was surprised when I first walked round the cemetery where Lina is buried by the number of young people who are buried there. We live in a society which has made such a taboo of death that we are hermetically sealed from its reality. I made friends with the parents of other young girls who died in their late teens and early twenties – what Anton refers to as my 'graveyard gang' – and I find myself seeking out their company. There is a way in which one doesn't have to explain oneself or translate anything – our loss is a 'given', and although the experience is unique to each, a sense of solidarity manages to penetrate the loneliness and isolation of grief.

Two things give me strength. One is human contact – actual touch, not just metaphorical embraces, though the knowledge that one is surrounded has its own consolation. Touch is hard to secure since I am not in a relationship, and harder still because the English are not a touchy-feely people. Nor is my family. But a hand held, or a hug shared, or even just the presence of living warmth, feeds a deep need in me. That last impression of Adelina's hand, cold, wet, profoundly alien, calls out to be counterbalanced with a humming, living touch.

The other source of strength is creativity. I am happiest when absorbed in writing or photography or even just in thinking and re-jigging my take on the world. Here again, creativity is something I find hard to accommodate, in this case for financial reasons, but something I am determined to fit into my life. Everything is transient, true, but the state of concentration attained while being creative stops time and thereby transcends transience – or seems to. And besides, the ludic dimension of creativity, which appeals to me hugely, makes fun of the very notion of permanence.

Which leads me to my last observation, also to do with time. For all the very welcome compassionate sympathy I have received, both from friends and from strangers, and for which I am genuinely grateful, I have come to recognise that our imaginations fall short in one essential dimension – the temporal one. Compassionate imagination allows people to dip – and to dip deeply – into grief, but (mercifully), it doesn't keep them there. Whereas living with loss means just that, an ongoing reality that lives with us and within us.

Bi Scott

Dreamland (excerpt)

She cannot see the grain
Ripening on hill and plain;
She cannot feel the rain
Upon her hand.
Rest, rest, for evermore
Upon a mossy shore;
Rest, rest at the heart's core
Till time shall cease:
Sleep that no pain shall wake;
Night that no morn shall break
Till joy shall overtake
Her perfect peace.

Christina Rossetti

154

Harry Charles Chappe Sidebottom

4 November 1974 –
5 September 1999

Harry

"God gives us love, someone to love he lends us"

Alfred Lord Tennyson

On 5th September 1999 at approximately 2am my son Harry Sidebottom, aged 24, had a fatal car accident. (I still can't say that 'died' word). I was on holiday in France when I got the call. Instant split-second shock horror, life suspending, never to be the same again; head jerking north to south, only a small dull thud of fear, quietly thumping as a mish-mash of rock metal in my head shrieked, 'No, no, no, not true, dear God, not true'.

It was at that time of year when the days of full-blown summer with leaves and grass still green seem exhausted; a nip in the air; a feeling of sunny days drawing to an end. How apt.

The trauma of returning to England from France in time to meet my daughter Lottie's flight home from Australia occupied my spaced-out thoughts. For several days thereafter Lottie, her father and I sat in crumpled heaps amongst the turmoil of redecoration in my house in London. Somehow this topsy-turvy mess brought a certain comfort, as if mirroring our inner chaos and numb-shattering grief.

Harry's tiny funeral for the three of us was conducted with terrifying calm on a sunny God-given day, his spirit soaring protectively high above us. Was this a charming celebration of a life too short-lived, or a vile ritual to test us further? Later that month we had a Thanksgiving Service (you can't really have a memorial for one so young). The church was full to bursting; it was a stupendous service but truly unbelievable to accept that it was organised for my darling son. 'Thank you very much for coming' I heard myself say to all the friends who arrived. What else do you say while contemplating the rest of your life without someone so loved?

'How can it be the end when it is just the beginning?' wrote Sophie Large. This was, after all, a new planet for me with no signposts for guidance. Brain, spirit and soul on massive overload, a total blank arrived and I don't remember much. Days passed in a grey, gelatinous, dour sort of way. When talking emotionally I would falter to a halt mid-sentence. Doing anything became the equivalent of climbing Everest. Lost son, marriage and home – a changed world indeed; and steamrollered as I was, I just longed to crawl into Harry's bed, throw away the key and say goodbye to the world. Harry gone, not here anymore – gone where? Australia perhaps? No, gone forever – inconceivable to comprehend, as I'm sure everyone in the same situation would agree. You have two choices though – to live or die yourself.

Eight years on, life is defined simply as Before Harry and After Harry. Before Harry holds a vision of happy, sunny days. After Harry – you've guessed it – pretty cloudy with dark threatening clouds hanging over my heart. I keep telling myself I can look at life and see all the annoyances and disasters, or I can appreciate little things that are always there for me. I suppose I have swapped the anaesthetic of eight years for an uneasy, begrudging acceptance of my loss. Something, though, is continually 'wrong' in my life and I can only explain it like this: you know how sometimes on waking you have an immediate sense of dread which stays with you until you identify the problem you face? Well, that is an everyday occurrence for me, a little diminished now, but still there. Mother Nature is no longer wrapping me in her protective mantle; thus I am, in times of stress, more thin-skinned, brittle and bruised than before. Perhaps the positive of this is an awareness and empathy, and an ability to communicate easily with others in their misfortunes.

Losing your only son wipes the meaning out of things and brings a weight of sadness so heavy at times that I can hardly bear it. The continuous feeling of raw isolation; the repercussions of disbelief as the shock horror comes careering round the corner, sometimes knocking me off my feet as I ask myself for the millionth time, has he really gone? The immense life-long regret at not being able to give my life for my son, not seeing his body, not deciding what clothes he should wear in that beastly coffin - these things will haunt me for the rest of my life. The wishing not to have to write this piece, as it is a further endorsement of the recognition that Harry really is not here. Limiting lifelong regrets is a major part of my advice now whenever I talk to newly bereaved people. Left with only a smiling photograph to fill this immense void, I have little unforced energy to spare for anything other than survival, and the occasional joie de vivre that pops up leaves me with a niggling guilt. Sometimes life seems insurmountable, other times I feel disconnected with only a 'walk-on' part in life.

The up-sides? After the mental torture, physical pain is of no consequence. Visiting a medium gives connection to my son and reassurance that his spirit is always with me. Knowing that nothing worse can happen is a weird sort of plus. Living with the pain means he is never forgotten. Harry has passed on to me some of his good bits: helping others in the same boat has come easily to me; seeing colour again instead of grey pervading everything. Someone once said the most you can hope to bequeath your children is roots and wings and maybe, just maybe I managed this. Our memories are their parting gift to us and these will never die. I'm fairly sure that Harry pressed the right lift button on leaving this world, and is now up in heaven as a Junior Personnel Manager, cajoling the 'young'.

I'm part of a jigsaw puzzle with the unlikelihood of the pieces ever totally fitting again. I could put on someone else's shoes and pretend, live another life and make choices that in reality I don't have. Have I moved on and let go a little? Perhaps. Has there been a tiny corner turned? Maybe. I view clichés like 'moving on' and 'letting go' as either an act of disloyalty or betrayal, or as a sign of no longer caring for my son – hence my reticence to admit to either.

The happy certainty though that Harry is often with me came a few weeks ago, when my daughter Lottie and newly-born grandson Jake were staying. As I was walking my dog Jambo one early morning, I looked up at the beautiful clear, crisp blue sky and saw it riddled with a hazy patchwork of kisses –xxxx. No amount of aeroplanes could have created that without a monstrous pile-up in the sky! Anyone who has read Le Petit Prince by Antoine St. Exupery will remember the piece where he looks up at the sky and sees kisses sent to him by his departed friend.

The arrival of my first grandchild (I also have eight gorgeous step-grandchildren) has endorsed the feeling of continuity in life. While I have lost my son, I am delighted to find myself welcoming this little treasure into the world with as much joy and verve as I do.

It's odd to say life is OK – almost good – yet at the same time carrying within the greatest pain. Harry is 'there', embedded within the souls of all those he loved, living in every breath we take, and mercifully the glimpses of memories that once used to slip just out of reach feel slightly more stable now. I feel he makes possible the vital link to connect emotionally with people once again.

I don't exactly see Harry's face, but I feel the warmth of his smile and hear the echo of his voice. He and I laugh together sometimes, and I kiss him, tell him I love him and that I always will...

Look to the sun, and let the shadows fall behind you...

Flappy Lane Fox

When Life is Not the Same

How do people act when they are around me?
It's hard to tell or sense, since I can't see.
I feel a coldness, an uncertainty, a wariness,
Could it have anything to do with my unhappiness?

They're all too frightened to mention to say,
How might I be feeling, or coping today.
I want them to go, no, I want them to stay,
Can never decide to tell them to go or stay.

How does life continue when life's turning around?
I permanently feel like I've been run aground.
The need to hide and the need to find peace
Is a feeling that I believe will never cease.

158

Everyone looks and everyone stares,
Not knowing the damaging effect of their glares.
I am changed forever, no doubt about that,
I feel I am forced to wear a 'misery hat'.

You want sympathy one minute, and not the next,
There's no code how to act, nothing written in text,
Is there formula on how life should or could be,
For one who is grieving, someone like me?

'Cos I know that he's here, all around in the air,
Relishing his fun up in his heavenly lair,
I just wish so hard, that I could get to see him,
But the light up there is faint and painfully dim.

Belief feels shaky, if it is there at all.
I've never really felt His strength or His call,
So who do I turn to now in my hour of need?
For my heart is so heavy and I can't stop the bleed.

I think of you always, in every ounce of my life,
Knowing full well you're there to enjoy both trouble and strife,
Just please stay there through all of my days,
As I need your guidance through my life's long gaze.

What I'm trying to say is that I'll love you always,
And that love won't diminish into a misty haze.
I feel your strength every second that I'm here,
And count on the fact that you'll always be near

Lottie Sidebottom

A Heartbeat Away

159

A Sparrow Fell

From Flappy to God

A sparrow fell – and no one heard.
Nobody cares. It was just a bird.
From all the numberless flitting throng,
Of sparrows, who would miss one song?
But God leaned down and whispered 'I care,
T'was one of my sparrows and I was there'.
Our Harry was killed, full of sunshine and laughter
Full of youthful wild times and some regrets later
And hurts to smooth over, and deeds to applaud
A young man fell; Where were you God?
A young man fell; Why weren't you there?
It is only for sparrows and such that you care?

If you're God at all – then you could have prevented
This nightmare of pain. So you must have consented.
I've always believed You were loving and good.
I'd like to still believe, if only I could.

But God, if you love me, how can you allow
Such unbearable pain as I'm feeling right now.
Such helplessness – hopelessness – bitter regret,
So many tears that have fallen and yet
So many more that are still locked inside.
Oh God – out there somewhere, have YOU ever cried?
I'm not even sure anymore, that you're real,
But if you are God, do you care how I feel?

From God to Flappy

Beloved I care, In the midst of your grief,
In the midst of your stricken and crumbling grief,
In the midst of the blackness and total despair,
In the midst of your questioning, child, I am there,
In the midst not far off, in some vague fifth dimension,
But there, where you are, giving you my attention.

My constant attention - and not just today.
Since before you were born, I have loved you this way.
You're important to me, every hair on your head.

I have numbered myself. Can these be tears that you shed
Go uncounted? Unnoticed? Nay, child, here I stand
Close enough that each teardrop falls into my Hand.
Nor am I stranger to anguish - to loss
My own Son was taken in one day - by a cross.
I know what you suffer, I know what you'll gain,
If you'll let me walk with you into your pain,
I'll carry your grief, and your sorrow I'll bear,
You've only to reach out your hand - I am there.
Let me walk with you now, through the long heavy days;

Let me slowly begin changing heartache to praise.
Take hold of my hand, child, take hold of my love.
I will lead you to joys that you yet know not of,
Your faith may be weak, and your trust incomplete,
But I'll not walk too fast for your stumbling feet.

Flappy Lane Fox

A Heartbeat Away

Abigail Slatter

9th February 1998

Abigail

A life not lost just held forever

We were trying for a baby and were so pleased when I fell pregnant really quickly with our first child. But at 23 weeks, I woke up on the Saturday morning feeling terribly unhappy and tearful. I just felt dreadful but didn't link this with the baby at all. Later that day we had friends to stay, and I just went through the motions. It was Sunday night that I realised I hadn't felt the baby moving, but thought that maybe because I had been distracted, I just hadn't noticed any movements.

On Monday morning I had to drive Simon to his new job in Reading, without telling him that the baby seemed too still. I then went straight to the doctors; by that time I knew I had definitely not felt the baby move. They couldn't find a heartbeat but said they often can't, so don't be too worried. They would send me to hospital to have a scan. The doctor was trying to be reassuring but I knew definitely then that our baby had died.

I drove to Wycombe Hospital on my own – I hadn't rung anyone yet just in case I was wrong. At the hospital, it was all a blur. During the scan I could see the screen and there was no heartbeat. No one was saying anything. I said, "The baby has died, hasn't it?" Someone said, "Well, we can't find a heartbeat" and I thought, "You just can't say it, can you?" It was as if the doctors thought they would be saving my feelings if no one used the word 'dead'.

It wasn't a shock because I think I had actually realised on Sunday. Outwardly I was very calm – I'm not a hysterical kind of person. I spoke to my best friend

162

Kim who I worked with and told her. That was really difficult. I can't recall the conversation with Simon - I don't even know if I rang him, or if Kim did. It was his first day at a new job and I didn't want to worry him. He was pulled out of his induction meeting to be told there was a call from the hospital.

I do remember needing the toilet. I was already in one of the labour rooms, with the bathrooms just outside the door, and the midwife made me leave the door half open. I sat there wondering if she thought I might collapse or if she were worried that I might try and do myself harm. I remember looking around the room wondering what on earth she thought I was going to hurt myself with. I don't think the realisation had hit me, stupid as it sounds, everything had stopped with the confirmation of the scan. MY BABY WAS DEAD. It didn't even occur to me that I still had to give birth, the situation wasn't just going to go away.

I was given the choice of going home and waiting for labour to start naturally, but to me that was only prolonging it and I didn't want to do that. I was given an injection to induce my labour, sometime around Monday lunchtime. Simon got there at some point - I can't remember. My midwife examined me and told me afterwards she thought I wouldn't have the baby until possibly Wednesday, but it was all very quick. I remember it being very, very painful and being told I could have diamorphine, which you can't normally have in labour because it affects the baby. When waiting for the next injection of pain relief, I thought, "I'll have an epidural next time." I was never in any doubt that I would have another child.

I always felt I was going to have a little girl and when I was laying on the trolley looking at the scan of my baby with no heartbeat, I heard the name 'Abigail', as clearly as if someone had said it. This wasn't a name that we had even considered, but I remember saying to Simon, "She's going to be a little girl and her name is Abigail."

I had her at 11.46pm and the midwife commented that she had a long umbilical cord and a small placenta. One would probably have been OK, but not both. After the birth I was very calm. I remember lying in the bed and they had taken Abigail away. I don't remember seeing her - they may have shown her to me, I don't know. If they had, I wasn't in a fit state to take it in.

A little while later our midwife asked if we wanted to see Abigail. She brought her to us, dressed her and put her in a Moses basket. She was 23½ weeks and was perfect. Her skin was translucent and she looked very red but otherwise perfect. I was surprised at that – I hadn't even tried to imagine it. I didn't realise how perfectly formed babies are. The midwife said she was a very long baby. They have since said that about Alexandra, my next baby, and it was a nice thought that she was like her sister – a family thing.

Simon was in a chair, and I was meant to be resting. I remember thinking, "I can't cope with this." In the space of a few hours I had gone from being an excited expectant mother to laying next to my stillborn daughter in a hospital bed. Two years before I had been at the mind, body and spirit exhibition in London. I attended a workshop about the fact that we have all actually chosen the life we are living and the tutor had made the point that 'Help is always there but you need to ask for it.' I lay in bed thinking, "I need help to deal with this." I suddenly felt totally calm as if injected with something – I had an image of a river and a figure on the far bank. The image faded and suddenly I felt calm; the situation was still dreadful, but I could deal with it.

The midwife spoke to us about what we might like to do, and we stayed with Abigail all day and night Tuesday and had her with us in the room. We held her and took photos. Our parents came down – it was awful for them, they had not only lost a grandchild but had to see us grieving as well. We had been given the option of taking Abigail home, but that would have been too hard. I couldn't do it because I knew I couldn't have kept her.

We were asked about having a post mortem to find out why our baby died and they also wanted to take blood from me. I knew they weren't going to find anything – it just happened and I was sure there was nothing wrong with Abigail or me. But we agreed to a post mortem. We were not forced in any sense, but I just wanted to confirm what I was thinking. We were told where she would be taken and how she would get there. We left the hospital on the Wednesday and Abigail was taken to Oxford for her post mortem. A couple of years later we learned that some samples, slides and part of her pancreas had been retained. Finding out opened up everything afresh, but we understood that the samples had been kept for research – there was no malicious intent to upset us. We had to decide if we wanted to have these parts re-buried with her, but the thought of this was too much to bear. We decided to leave them with the hospital.

While in hospital the chaplain asked if we would like to see her. Neither of us is religious, but we agreed and Julie was so nice, we were really glad. She blessed Abigail and gave us a little blessing card, and we asked if she would do the funeral. We went to a local funeral directors in Thame – at 28, I didn't know how to arrange a funeral. You don't think you're going to have to do it. They had had training from the Child Bereavement Charity and were brilliant. They gave us the opportunity to put things in her casket; I chose a rabbit I had as a child and a photo of Simon and I. My father is a wood turner and turned a rattle and my mother wrote her name in pastels and decorated it. I took everything along and assumed I would hand them over to be placed with Abigail, but the lady said, "Your daughter is in there, you can go and put it in yourself if you want to." I was shocked and a bit scared, but didn't know how to say no.

Being in the room with Abigail brought it right back, she was in the coffin, but all wrapped up so I couldn't see any of her. Although it was hard at the time, I was really pleased to have done it. I only had my baby for a very short time, and wanted to do the best for her while I could. Then, on the day of the funeral, I didn't think I could get in the car with her coffin. I suddenly panicked and thought, "I don't want to do this." My parents and Simon's parents were there but I can hardly remember it. We had a reading at the graveside by Khalil Gibran which really rang true for me –

> 'When you are sorrowful, look again in your heart and you shall see that in truth you are weeping for that which has been your delight.'

Abigail is buried in the churchyard in Thame. I couldn't cremate her – it felt too violent to me. We have since had two more daughters, Alexandra and Eleanor and we take them there and they know all about her. I don't do it regularly as I'd feel guilty if missed a week, but it's nice to have somewhere to go.

When you find out that the baby you are carrying has died, it's as if your whole world stops. When I came home from hospital I was shocked when my milk started coming through – nobody had warned me. Because Abigail hadn't been full term I had assumed my body would somehow know that she wouldn't need feeding. It's so unfair – yet another constant, painful reminder of what has happened. With my later pregnancies I produced so much milk that I froze it and gave it to the baby unit. Babies at 24 weeks can survive but often there's nothing to feed them if their mums don't produce enough milk. I liked the fact my milk went to the hospital to help other babies her age.

Simon only had a week off. He had just started new job. When you have to earn money, what can you do? My company was very good and allowed me to take as much time off as I needed. It was so difficult when people would ring up to chat - they wouldn't know then I'd have to tell them. You do get people avoiding you, but I can understand that because what can they say? People sent flowers, which was really nice; it acknowledged Abigail's existence which was so important.

I was at home, very upset. There's a line in a Sheryl Crow song that sums up that period of time -'I feel like a stranger in my own life'. You still look the same in the mirror, you're living in the same house, have the same friends but nothing is ever, ever going to be the same. I made myself get up, get dressed, and lived on chardonnay (only a couple of glasses!) and chocolate Aero. I didn't want to get out of bed or go out of the house, but knew that I had to. At least I could stay at home; Simon had to go to work each day and deal with clients. Grieving dads of stillborn babies aren't afforded the same sympathy as mums; everyone thinks that as the woman has actually had to give birth then she must be suffering more. Certainly that's true physically, but women don't have the monopoly on grief.

I had panic attacks. I forgot how to use my cash point card; I needed money and had a total blank. I couldn't remember my number, put the card back in my purse and walked away. If I went shopping, I only bought a couple of items at a time, scared I would get flustered if they whizzed them through the checkout quickly and I couldn't pack and would cry. I really didn't want to cry in public, not like that. It was worse for Simon, who was out on the road a lot. He wanted to be with me but couldn't. We reacted differently - he'd see people with a baby and think "Why them and not us?" I have never felt we were being punished. Everything happens for a reason and it happened.

We had been offered support by CBC. I was sceptical of how talking to someone could possibly make things better, but it did. I wanted to try for another baby straight away. I was worried that I would be so elated my grief would be on hold and would lie in wait. But I was pregnant by April and with support, I managed. It worked for us. I had thought initially, "I am not buying anything for this baby" but then someone asked me how I would feel if it happened again and I hadn't bought anything for this baby while it was alive. I thought, "You're right. If this baby does die I'll think 'I didn't buy it a thing'."

166

When I was pregnant with Alexandra, I wouldn't listen to the heartbeat. I'd let them listen, but didn't want to hear it. The first five months of pregnancy was like "I have been here before" and seemed to take forever. Wycombe Hospital was brilliant and very cautious with me during pregnancy. I had Alexandra in the December after Abigail died. She was born with a hole in the heart, but I wasn't worried about it, I just knew she was going to be fine. I've never been over-anxious as a mother, even though people thought I would have been. You need to trust your instinct; mothers know a lot.

We'd always wanted two children. I'm very open with the girls and we have photos of Abigail around the house. The flip side is you have to be prepared for their questions. Aged 8 and 5, I've had to field questions such as "Is she just a skeleton now? "Did you want her to die?" You have to be prepared for their questions but I would rather have that than the children not knowing Abigail existed.

When Abigail first died it is always there in front of your face, all seeing, all thinking, all consuming. You either go on or don't. You have to have faith that it's not going to be that awful forever. Gradually, instead of being right in front of your face it moves next to you. Everything I do in life, she is there with me.

When people said "I bet you wish you had never got pregnant" I had to say "No, I wish Abigail hadn't died but I don't wish her away." I'm glad I had her.

I believe Abigail is always with us. I have always believed that when people die, their spirit is still around. For some reason Abigail needed to be born; I don't understand why but it happened for a reason. I'm happy to accept that.

In 2004 I started going to meditation lessons to learn how to relax - the tutor used to lead me into a state of relaxation, then at the end ask me about what I had experienced and interpret it and discuss it with me. On numerous occasions I haven't mentioned something that I considered unimportant, only to have her mention it, and in great detail. I don't know how she could do this, but just accepted that somehow she seems to tune in to what I am experiencing. After this particular session however, before I starting recounting what I had experienced, she said she couldn't wait to tell me something that had happened, as she had never seen anything like it before. She said that as soon as the session started, a little girl aged about 7 came into the room, climbed onto my lap, put her arms around me and hugged me for the entire session. She said the love emanating from her was incredible and that in her years of doing this she had never had this happen before. I promptly burst into tears, and after a while explained to her about Abigail (who I'd never mentioned before), and that today was the 7th anniversary of her birth. During the session I had no awareness of this, but to me it just confirms that Abigail is always with me.

Darryl Slatter

I'm not going to try and comfort you,
I know I couldn't.
But try to remember that the
goodness of a child can never die.
You will continue to experience
this goodness many times.
You will experience it in the streets.
You will experience it in the houses,
in all the places of the town.
It will be in the vineyards and the orchards,
in the rivers and the clouds, in all the things that make this
a world for us to live in.
You will experience this goodness
in all things that are here out of love,
and for love – all the things that are abundant,
all the things that grow.
A child may leave – or be taken away –
But the goodness of a child stays.
It stays forever.
Love is immortal and makes all things immortal.

William Saroyan

Callum David Anders Smith

5 June 1998 – 12 June 1999

Callum

The summer of 1998 was one of the happiest of my life. My husband Campbell and I were living in a small town in Sweden and we were expecting our first child. Life was so simplistic and our needs were few.

After an uncomplicated pregnancy and birth, our son Callum arrived at 3.45am on 5th June 1998, weighing 8lb 11oz. The Swedish midwives were amazing, making the whole experience a very special one. They delivered Callum straight onto my chest and wrapped him quickly into a blanket. The first moment I looked at my son will stay in my memory forever. He was a fairly big baby, all pink and round, and he was alert. As I looked at his little face, his eyes locked onto mine and I felt our souls touch. I watched Campbell hold his son for the first time and I knew he was just as bowled over as I was. After the doctor had checked Callum over, we were reassured that he was a perfectly healthy baby, although he did have a large lump on his leg. The lump itself was completely benign and would probably disappear as he grew into boyhood. Obviously, I would have rather the lump not be there, but I was not unduly concerned.

After a three-night stay in hospital, we returned home, a happy family of three. Our parents came out for an extended visit and we were proud to show off their new grandson. Since moving to Sweden we had built up a large circle of friends, mainly ex-pats who also had small children and newborns of their own. My life soon settled into a daily routine of trips into town with the baby or long walks with other mums. Callum was such a good baby, and would

169

often sleep for hours in the pram, waking only for a feed and a cuddle. He certainly liked to feed and was growing rapidly. Everything seemed to be as it should be. However, a tiny voice at the back of my mind began to tell me something was wrong – I just didn't know what.

To begin with, Callum seemed to be unusually still. He was naturally a very calm, passive baby, but where my friends' babies were often kicking their legs, Callum would lie, unmoving. When he was 9 weeks old, I remember asking my Mum at what age babies start to kick – I really had no idea. Because my Mum was back home in England, she couldn't see for herself the reason for my concern, but she knew I was worried. I began to think that the lump on his leg was perhaps too heavy for him to lift his leg and we did consult a Paediatrician in Sweden. He reassured me that the lump was benign, but treated me like an over-anxious first-time Mum. I decided to investigate having the lump removed when we returned to England for a holiday in the October.

Our trip home in October was a great success. Callum was christened alongside his cousin, Liam, and all our family were there. Campbell and I then travelled up to Scotland, to show off our new son to the Scottish side of the family. While we were up there, I arranged to see a Paediatrician in England before we returned to Sweden, to talk about the lump. By the time of the appointment, Campbell had run out of holidays and had to return to work, so my parents came with me. The Paediatrician was lovely and confirmed that the lump was benign, but he listened carefully to my concerns about Callum's lack of movement. He confirmed that Callum's muscle tone seemed to be a little undeveloped but felt that this was unrelated to the lump on his leg. I felt, for the first time, that someone finally understood my concerns. The Paediatrician suggested we consult a neurologist, "just to rule out anything sinister."

We managed to secure an appointment that day with a neurologist at the Portland Hospital and were sent for a variety of tests, including a blood sample. We were told to come back the next day for the results, but the doctor did say that he was very worried about Callum. He believed that Callum had a condition know as Spinal Muscular Atrophy Type 1. I had never heard of it and wasn't prepared at that time to ask too many questions. I would see what the tests revealed. I spoke to Campbell in Sweden that night and he said he would look it up on the Internet. I still didn't want to know.

The following day, I returned to London with my parents for the results. The face of the neurologists told us immediately that the matter was very serious, but I was still not prepared for what he was to tell me. After a brief greeting, he simply told us that there was no way he could soften the news. Callum did in fact have SMA Type 1. He went on to explain that this was a muscle-wasting disease and the average life expectancy of an infant was 9 months. Most would not see their 1st Birthday. Gradually, all the muscles would weaken, including the respiratory muscles, and the baby would die of respiratory failure. He went on to advise that we should never put Callum on a respirator, as we would not be able to take him off. While we sat there in shock, he also explained that this condition was a genetic one, carried on a recessive gene from both parents. Therefore, we stood a 1 in 4 chance of each pregnancy being affected with the condition. I heard my parents gasp at the news and all the while the doctor was watching me, concerned about my reaction. I waited for one to come, but I think I was so numb that nothing happened. I remember asking if he would suffer and was reassured that he needn't.

The journey home was a long and silent one. No one knew what to say to each other. The only person unaffected by the news was Callum himself, who of course had not changed. He needed feeding, changing and loving in just the same way. I instinctively felt that I could not fall apart because my baby needed me - and therefore I didn't. My telephone conversation with Campbell later that night was extremely painful. I only had to confirm what the diagnosis was and he knew from his own research what the outcome was going to be. Campbell broke down on the phone and my heart went out to him. He was all alone, in a different country with his family in crisis elsewhere. We couldn't even hold each other. He arranged to fly back to England the next day.

After a few days, we decided to return to Sweden, pack up all our things and come back home. If Callum's life was going to be a short one, we felt that he had a right to know his family and they him. We returned to the UK in December and moved back into our own house in January 1999. Despite the desperate prognosis, life settled into some kind of routine. The support I received from our GP and Health Visitor was fantastic. We couldn't have coped without them. As Callum grew, he eventually needed a suction machine and was put onto a sleep apnoea monitor at night. I also received regular visits from the local child physiotherapist and was put in touch with the children's section of a local Hospice at Home service. It was the hospice staff who later became my lifeline.

In spite of everything, Callum remained quite well and was a very happy, contented baby. He loved to be held in my arms and was always smiling and laughing. He also loved to eat and was never happier than when he was sticking his fingers into chocolate pudding or custard. Swimming was his favourite activity. We had decided at an earlier stage that we would not live with "SMA" and would treat Callum as normally as possible. As he grew, his lack of muscle tone became more obvious. He was never able to roll over, hold his head up on his own or sit unaided. We were issued with a "snug seat" which allowed him to sit in an upright position, and he could interact with the world around him. Although we never took Callum to places where he may pick up a cold or respiratory infection, he had lots of opportunities to meet people and he touched the hearts of everyone he met. Every now and then I would catch him watching me with a clear and unwavering gaze. It was such a strange, mature look to see in a baby and I always felt that he knew something I didn't.

In February 1999, Callum had his first respiratory arrest while we were visiting friends in Derby. Following a cold, he simply stopped breathing one night and Campbell and I had to resuscitate him before the ambulance arrived. We were rushed to Derby Children's Hospital where they managed to treat his chest infection and therefore prolong his life. However, we knew that we had been given a taster of what was to come. After our trip to Derby, each month or special occasion became a milestone for us. First it was Mothers' Day, then it was Campbell's Birthday. Finally a day that we thought we would never celebrate arrived: Callum's 1st Birthday. Friends and family came from far and wide to celebrate with us. It was a magical day and it seemed he could live forever. Everyone cried when we sang 'Happy Birthday' except Callum, who spent the entire party smiling and playing with a balloon. Campbell and I were especially happy because we were harbouring a secret from everyone; I was newly pregnant with our second child and had just been for a CVS test to confirm that the baby was not affected with SMA.

Sadly, five days after Callum's birthday, my GP phoned to say that our new baby was also affected with SMA and offered the choice of a termination. Although Campbell and I had not had many deep discussions about this subject, we both knew that we could not bring another baby into this world with this dreadful condition. I was admitted to our local hospital that night, scheduled for a termination in the morning. I remember crying throughout the night, but still my main focus was Callum. After the operation, I was awoken by a beautiful nurse who told me my little boy had been brought in to hospital. My first thought was "How nice" but she soon explained that Callum was having trouble breathing.

Within 20 minutes of waking up, I was wheeled down to the children's ward, where Callum was in full respiratory arrest. Campbell was in tears, not being able to believe we could lose two children within the same hour. The hospital staff worked extremely hard to stabilize Callum, determined that he would not die until I was there. Their efforts were rewarded when Callum began to breathe on his own again and he was placed in my arms. I remember feeling extremely calm, despite sitting in a wheelchair in only a theatre gown. One of the nurses dashed back to my ward to collect my clothes and I stayed with Callum for the rest of the day.

That day and the night that followed was long and hard. Although Callum was breathing on his own, it was obviously difficult and he was given tranquilizers so he would not become distressed. In a very calm manner, the Paediatrician outlined the situation for us. Callum would continue to stop breathing and we had to consider how long we could prolong his suffering. Campbell and I just looked at each other and I said, "We have to let him go". Campbell agreed. My parents arrived during the day and we explained the situation.

At lunchtime the following day, Callum went into full respiratory failure again and despite the best efforts of the nurses, it was obvious to us that he needed to go. So we asked for his resuscitation to be stopped. He was placed in our arms and as he slowly slipped away we told him that it was OK for him to go, that we loved him and would never forget him. We stayed holding him for some time afterwards. My parents arrived and also held him to say good-bye. We had decided that one of the hospice nurses would take him to the local undertakers that afternoon, as we couldn't bear to put him in the hospital morgue. Walking out of the hospital without Callum was extremely difficult, but we were not able to cry. Throughout the following week, we were busy making arrangements for his funeral, informing our family and friends of his death, but still we couldn't cry. It wasn't until a few weeks later, on a much-needed holiday, that I finally did cry. Campbell was still strong and silent.

From the moment Callum was diagnosed, I knew I would one day have to grieve, but I was not prepared for the depth of emotions that this would involve, or that Campbell and I would not be able to grieve together. We have never been a couple who have long in-depth discussions about things and this included our feelings over Callum's death. I needed to talk about him and about how I felt, but Campbell just couldn't. Although, he has always been able to talk about Callum, his feelings are a whole different matter. I did begin to feel resentful towards him as I felt isolated in my grief. I knew Campbell loved Callum just as much as I did and he was in just as much pain, but we couldn't talk about it together. It wasn't until a few months later when I was introduced to the Child Bereavement Charity that I began to understand how men and women often grieve in different ways.

Understanding that Campbell's need to restore our lives was his way of coping possibly saved our relationship. As I grew stronger, I understood that it was OK for me to deal with Callum's death my way and to let Campbell deal with it in his. Of course, it would have been easier for me if we could have talked, but not for Campbell. During the following two years, our lack of communication sorely tested me as we suffered three miscarriages and two failed attempts at a form of IVF treatment (known as PGD) where the genetic material is extracted from a fertilized egg to test for SMA. However, the understanding I gained from the bereavement support I had saved not only my marriage, but my sanity. It would be wrong for me to say that all understanding was on my part. I must have been very difficult to live with at times, particularly when I needed to just stay put and wallow in my grief for a while. Campbell never complained; it was just too painful for him to join in.

It is now over 8 years since Callum's death and our subsequent losses. However, I am very pleased to say that life is finally good once more. Almost exactly three years from the day Callum died, our second son Benjamin was born and was rapidly followed 16 months later by his younger brother Alastair. Both boys are unaffected by SMA and are thriving. Our household is noisy, often untidy, but is filled with laughter and joy. Both boys know that they have a brother who lives with God in Heaven and Ben considers himself to be an expert on this matter. Not a day goes past when Callum is not mentioned or thought about. His is a living memory in our lives, and we have a number of photographs of him amongst those of the other two; however we have taken care not to create a shrine in the house.

We are living proof that although life can throw you devastating blows, it will right itself in time. For Campbell and I, Ben and Alastair are simply the light at the end of a very long tunnel.

Heather Smith

Guy Sobel

23 September 1975 –
3 February 1994

Guy was the light of my life, and at the same time he proved to be a challenge for us all. He had a borderline mild learning disability, brought on by untreated infant jaundice. In the end though, it was the child-like innocence that resulted from his condition that was to be his saving grace, and subsequently ours too...

Guy was loving, kind, compassionate, and in many ways, hugely capable and resourceful. He was a keen sportsman, excelling at swimming and cycling, whilst flourishing at his school amongst his peers. He was very good with his hands, and could take a clock to pieces in minutes. He had huge charm, and tremendous insight, making observations on occasions that simply took my breath away. He had lovely manners, and always tried to please. One of his great compensations in life was that he was tall and extremely handsome, and this always stood him in good stead in his life... he was just so appealing!

Unfortunately Guy's father and I divorced in the early 80s. Consequently for 4 years, until I re-married, Guy and I along with his older sister became a very tight-knit little family entity. I doted on both children, and tried to be the best mother (and father) I could be.

In 1991, two years after I re-married, Guy complained about back pain. I took him to the GP who diagnosed some muscular mishap, and sent me to a rheumatologist. She took one look at Guy, and promptly sent us to the local

175

Nuffield hospital for a thorough check-up. Guy spent a few days there having various tests, and finally we had the dreadful news broken to us: he had cancer, specifically a Ewing's Sarcoma in the 4th vertebrae, inoperable, but to be treated with a combination of radiotherapy and chemotherapy. The surgeon who broke the news to us told us that he wanted Guy to be treated on the NHS, and that there was a new ground-breaking teenage cancer ward just opened in the Central Middlesex Hospital in London, and that we were to go there post haste.

We were told that Guy was to have chemo for a year, and then a course of radiotherapy. Guy settled into the pattern of having his chemo once every 3 weeks, staying on the ward for 3 days at a time. It became a way of life for us, a new reality. When he was at home, he would continue with his sports, going swimming and riding his bike with a vengeance. He was being tutored at home in between chemo sessions, as his low white blood count, peculiar to chemo, basically meant that he couldn't be amongst groups of people without risk of infection.

After a year of treatment, Guy was given the all-clear, and we took him to Disneyland in Florida for a wonderful holiday, which we all thoroughly enjoyed. In retrospect, I am so thrilled that we were able to share that experience.

Three months later, the cancer returned, and again Guy had to go through more treatment. Guy went through all his horrible chemo and radiotherapy without a single word of complaint. He just knuckled down and got on with it. His slight learning disability, I believe, made him less aware of how frightening his condition was... and instead of agonising over his situation, he just re-adjusted to his new reality.

At hospital though, things were not going so well. After a few months of treatment, the nursing staff wanted to tell Guy that it hadn't been successful, and that he was probably going to die. They insisted on carrying out their policy of being 'honest' with the patients. I passionately felt that this wasn't the right thing to do, and called a multi-disciplinary meeting, where I INSTRUCTED the staff to carry out my wishes as Guy's mother, or I would take him home. Reluctantly they complied with my instructions, but it gave me enormous stress, stress I could have done without. During Guy's treatments in hospital, I never once had trouble from him, but I had a lot of trouble with the hospital staff for two good reasons. Firstly, in hospitals staff can become inured to suffering. It doesn't affect them the way it affects us... they see too much of it. It is therefore very rare to find compassion in hospitals. Secondly, hospitals take away your control.

After the second course of chemo finished, Guy's specialist confirmed to me that the treatment hadn't been successful and that he probably wouldn't live to see Xmas. We then brought him home. I wanted his last few months to be filled with love and joy as much as possible. Over the course of the subsequent six months, Guy lost the use of his legs and was wheelchair-bound and doubly incontinent, but even this he faced with humour and acceptance.

I had a wonderful team of nurses and carers from various organisations come into our home to look after Guy's needs: my fabulous GP, the Marie Curie nurses, the Macmillan nurses along with a superb counsellor, and finally the wonderful Ian Rennie Hospice at Home team. I informed the teams that I did not believe in life at any cost, and that my main objective and top priority was to keep Guy pain-free and comfortable. Because I was having Guy nursed in our home, the various teams respected my wishes and indeed the Ian Rennie nurses, who were our prime support, were grateful to me that I spelled out exactly what my aims and objectives were.

We knew Guy was going to die, and I had a lovely lady minister I had met come round to see him weekly for six months to get to know him, so that at his funeral the Minister taking the funeral would have known him, and wouldn't be just talking about a stranger she had never met.

I talked about his death with him quite openly, and explained how he would be buried, not cremated, as I needed a headstone and grave to visit. He was quite practical about all of this and it was my husband and I who broke down, but never Guy. Somehow, and I don't know where he got this from, he firmly believed he was going to come back as a bird. Nothing could move him on this.

He told me he never wanted me to forget him.

As if I could.

I made sure that Guy was happy and comfortable right to the end. In the last few months, I yearned for his death as a release from all of this horror.... and I have to live with that every day of my life.

Finally, he died a peaceful death with our favourite nurse, Mary from the Ian Rennie team, myself and my husband holding hands round his bed. Contrary to the specialist's prediction, he did see Christmas... his last one, and he died in the February.

It had been raining heavily, but when he died that day on February 3rd at 10.45, the sun suddenly came out.

He's at peace now.

Epilogue:
In retrospect, there is one modicum of comfort that I have held onto through all the hard years of grief that I have gone through: I know in my heart of hearts that I did the very best for Guy. I couldn't have done more. More importantly though, Guy died knowing that I love him more than life itself...

...because I had the time to tell him.

Micki Aston

We Will Remember

They shall not grow old, as we that are left grow old:
Age shall not weary them nor the years condemn.
At the going down of the sun, and in the morning,
We will remember them.

Laurence Binyon

178

Betsy Louise and William John Woodbridge

2 August 2002 –
27 September 2004

Betsy and William

Paul and I have been married for 10 years this year, and we have been truly blessed to have 6 children between us.

Paul has a son Ben from his previous marriage who is now nearly 14 years old and very much a part of our family as we share custody of him. Ben is a very gentle, caring boy. He is handsome, kind and intelligent. He has a really big smile and shining eyes. He is an exceptionally fantastic and loving older brother to his younger siblings. It is wonderful to watch him gradually approach a stage in his life where he is growing with more emotional and physical maturity. He is not a difficult child in his teenage years; of course he has his moments but they are few and far between. He loves the usual things that boys of his age do, basketball, fishing, table tennis, music, golf, but of course girls are an absolute no no! He also loves his Dad.

A year after we were married, along came our first child together, Lily, our darling little girl whom we adored from the second she arrived screaming into the world! She is such a character, bright, beautiful and bursting with brilliant energy that is so innocent. She is our friend. She portrays an inner strength and emotional maturity beyond her years. Lily is happy, spirited, bright, vibrant, naughty, loving, kind, quirky and makes us all laugh. She is such a chatterbox and so much fun.

Paul and I had always hoped for a large family. Lily had been such a joy and a real character and such an easy baby that when we discovered I was

179

expecting twins when Lily was 14 months old, we were completely thrilled and over the moon. I just could not believe how lucky I was and I would savour every single moment of this amazing privilege.

Pregnancy itself is such an amazing experience, but the discovery of expecting twins is simply unique. Carrying two babies is simply wonderful; two heart beats, two lots of kicks in your tummy, and two extra stone around your bottom!

Betsy Louise and William John arrived six weeks prematurely on the 2nd of August 2002 by caesarean section at Wexham Park Hospital, Slough and they were tiny. They were small but fortunately not poorly, so they had to stay in special care to grow and learn to feed before they were allowed home a month later. The staff at Wexham Park were absolutely wonderful and we feel humbled by the devotion and care that they gave to every baby in the unit.

The first night at home, I think that Paul and I managed to have forty minutes of sleep between us! Soon however we had sorted a really good system of feeding and within 4 months we had two babies sleeping for 12 hours a night – thank goodness!

Over the next two years we just bumbled along as a really, really happy family. Of course there were times when it was really hard looking after three small children under three, but we stuck to a very good routine and therefore reaped the benefits of three wonderful, happy and confident children. Lily and William had formed a very special bond and simply adored each other. They had big smiling faces, and wonderful extrovert, outgoing, cheeky characters. William had a mop of curly, blond, bouncy hair, dancing blue eyes and chunky short legs. He loved his little life, and his very pink bear that he dragged everywhere with him. He loved to dance and jump and roll. He adored mushrooms and his cot, swimming and being dressed up by the girls in shocking pink feather boas. Betsy had developed into an independent, clever little girl, who gave her affection carefully, but secretly loved everyone to bits, particularly her Daddy. She had piercing blue eyes that smiled at your eyes when she looked at you, and an aura of calm and peace surrounding her. She loved her nurses dressing up outfit, she also loved mushrooms and spaghetti carbonara and chocolate, climbing up the slide, pottering about, hitting Lily, doing ballet in her tutu and she absolutely hated having her hair cut.

180

Ben would come over at weekends and for school holidays and we would just all enjoy the simple things in life together. Teddy bear picnics in the garden, sand sandwiches at the beach, ice cold sprinklers whizzing around the grass, buckets and spades, camps, shepherds pie, little faces smeared with ice cream, hide and seek, the smell of sun kissed skin, bare bottoms, dancing shows, a house with the sound of happiness and laughter, bubbly baths and clean pyjamas, bedtime stories and kisses goodnight, tales of tomorrow and dreams of yesterday.

Of course things were not always perfect because, like all young children, they did at times drive us both bonkers!

On occasions, Paul and I would sit in our garden and thoughtfully look at our idea of Perfect, our children running around playing and laughing, our strong marriage and the love we had for one another, and the love of wonderful friends and family. How and when did it get this good? We would both get that really warm, bubbly, bursting feeling of happiness in the pit of our stomachs to the extent that we would look at each other with tears brimming in our eyes.

For as long as I can remember, since a very young child, I had wanted to be a mother and now I had been blessed with three of the most beautiful children, who I loved and cherished so much that my heart would sometimes hurt. We all had a unique friendship that ran so deeply, respectfully and so strongly together, that it was at times overpowering. I felt like a lioness, bursting with pride over her three cubs.

Paul is a wonderful father, totally committed to his family, and completely involved in every aspect of their upbringing. Every evening in the summer, he would take them on an adventure to the tree house at the bottom of the garden whilst I cleaned up after supper, and then take them all up for a bath. He crawls around in the playroom, pretending to be a big friendly lion, flies kites, stands on side lines, makes really good sand castles, cooks a dad-like fry up on a Sunday morning, rubs their foreheads in a special way when they are ill. He loves all of his children, completely, honestly and truly.

In the spring of 2004 I found out that I was pregnant again; we were overjoyed. The twins would be going to nursery later that year and Lily would start at school, so it would be wonderful to have another baby at home to nurture.

In September 2004, Lily did start at school. Full time. She hated it! I would have to peel her off my trousers in the classroom every morning for what seemed liked weeks. I would phone my mum in tears after dropping her off and asking if home governors still existed! Of course three weeks later Lily settled into school and would skip in to class full of beans. I did find emotionally hard the separation that school brought, but it did however allow more individual time with the twins and also allow Lily to develop new friendships away from her siblings.

On the 27th September, just another ordinary Monday and four weeks after Lily had finally settled at school, I had arranged for my mum to come over after lunch so we could take Betsy and William out to the park, and then on to pick up Lily from school. I was by now seven and a half months pregnant and any extra help was truly cherished. When my mum arrived, the twins were still in bed having their lunchtime nap, so I suggested that we go and wake them together. On my way upstairs, I said to my mum, "Gosh it's really quiet, I think Betsy and William are still asleep. I was going to stop this nap tomorrow, but perhaps they do still need it". When I opened the door to their bedroom my life as I knew it, the life that I cherished and loved, the life that made me feel safe, secure and happy, disappeared.

Betsy and William had, for the second time in their lives, climbed out of their cots and had a fantastic time playing in their bedroom. There were clothes, baby wipes, cream, books, and toys everywhere. They had spent a lovely time dressing and undressing each other. Betsy had climbed into the bottom drawer of their large solid, antique chest of drawers to get some more clothes for William; tragically her weight had pulled the piece of furniture down on to them, which killed them both instantly. I tried desperately to resuscitate my two beautiful, perfect children but failed and they died.

Sirens, blue lights, screaming, green uniforms, ambulances, police cars, radio noise, paramedics, doctors, helicopter, confusion, hushed voices, tubes, machines, bleeping and then nothing. Silence.

They were two years old.

Nothing compares to child bereavement.

It is the single most painful, bewildering and agonizing emotion that any parent can experience. How on earth were Paul and I supposed to survive without two of our beloved children, our twins, our darling, darling twins?

182

Shattered, destroyed, sheer panic, racing heart, rising nausea in your throat, gasping for breath, petrified.

The enormity of grief, desperation and utter disbelief is incomprehensible. You are suddenly thrust on this journey of pain and loss beyond imagination, that you have absolutely no experience of. At times, Paul and I thought that the physical and emotional pain that we were living in would kill us. We were surviving second by second. Surely no human can survive with such extreme emotion; I felt that I was being constantly tortured. A close circle of wonderful friends and family supported us, and looked after us to the best of their ability, rocking and cradling our broken hearts for hours and hours, even though they themselves were at times paralysed through their own grief.

Merely functioning, five weeks after Betsy and William died I gave birth to our beautiful daughter Fleur. The depth and love we automatically had for Fleur was instinctive, and she has in many ways contributed to our survival.

She has grown into an incredibly loving child, who loves anything pink or purple. She adores the musical 'Annie', and is spellbound by Tikabilla. She loves lipstick, dollies, kisses and cuddles. She loves ballet, her snugly cows, nursery, strawberries and yellow peppers with a passion. She is very, very sweet and gentle, pretty and shy, loving and adorable. She fills our hearts with warm love and joy, and she was given to us when we needed her the most.

We have so far endured nearly four years without our beloved Betsy and William, but it has been a journey of pure determination, courage, discovery, dignity, absolute love for our children and the ability to discover an inner strength that we did not know existed. We have all had to endure a physical and emotional pain on a level that is indescribable, but we have remained united in our grief as a family, and have chosen to go on this journey together, honestly and forever.

Last year we were again blessed to have another gorgeous daughter, Poppy Eliza. She is naughty, shouty, beautiful, full of mischief, and her smile can light up a room; we all simply adore her.

We will never fully recover from losing our two darling children, Betsy and William, how could we, but we will also certainly not abandon them in their death, so we keep their memory very much in our day to day lives. They will never be forgotten. Ever. The children are not inhibited by their grief on a daily basis, but there are times when they feel really, really sad and miss them dreadfully. It is heartbreaking to witness but with lots of love, cuddles and reassurance, it passes in its own time. We have taught them to verbalise their inner emotions and assured them that we will be honest to the best of our ability with any concerns or questions they have at anytime. We have no secrets. We all grieve very openly and together and therefore hope and pray that they will not be further damaged emotionally through their bereavement.

It has been such hard, hard work with the complexities of our grief ever changing, but we are very slowly and gently learning to rebuild our lives without Betsy and William's physical presence; however there is never a moment in our day where Paul and I do not grieve for them. We have learnt to live as near to being a normal family as possible, being really brave and biting the inside of our mouths when the tears spring into our eyes, living with a constant pain in our hearts. But ultimately we just want our children to have a normal and happy childhood, so we combine all our efforts into providing a safe, secure and happy environment for them to thrive in. School runs, ballet, homework, sports day, Sunday roasts, dinner parties, Tescos, holidays, playgroups, X Factor, walking the dogs, discos, cuddles, laughter, smiles, sleepovers, more nappies and loads of love. But sadly it is now with such heavy, broken hearts and with two little people missing that Paul and I have learnt to manage our lives again.

Our living children, Ben, Lily, Fleur and Poppy remain our constant inspiration, we are without doubt so very proud of all of their achievements and their ability to have developed into such wonderful individuals, despite having experienced such trauma at such a young age.

As for Paul and I, well our lives have changed irreversibly but thankfully we love each other hugely, with a great depth and completely. We have a very deep, mutual respect for each other's bereavement, which is equal and without question, and ultimately we are the only two people in this world that really truly understand what the other feels. We are simply not prepared to do this without each other. We need to complete this journey together, sharing our love and cherished memories of all of our children and grow old together, supporting each other's hearts every step of the way.

We both miss Betsy and William with every single breath that we take.

Louise Woodbridge

Organisations that can help

Child Bereavement Charity

Tel: 01494 446648
Web: www.childbereavement.org.uk

The Child Bereavement Charity provides resources and support for families when a baby or child dies, and when children are bereaved of someone important in their life. The Charity operates a confidential Support and Information Line for families (9am to 5pm, Monday to Friday) which offers support through listening and signposting to helpful resources and relevant organisations, and a Family Bereavement Support Service.

The Charity's website at www.childbereavement.org.uk includes a range of helpful information and a discussion forum for families to share their experiences and support each other.

The charity offers a Buckinghamshire based Bereavement Support Service for families where a baby or child has died or where children and young people are bereaved. The service provides a range of responses including:

- telephone support and guidance on particular areas of concern for families either pre-bereavement, in the immediate aftermath of a death or in the longer term
- individual, couple and family support sessions
- parents' support groups for baby and child death
- Young People's Advisory Group
- groups for bereaved children with their surviving parent/carer

The Child Bereavement Charity also offers a comprehensive training and consultancy programme on all aspects of grief and bereavement.

Further information is available from our website or by contacting training@childbereavement.org.uk.

ARC (Antenatal Results and Choices)

Tel: 0207 631 0285
Web: www.arc-uk.org

ARC is the only national charity which provides non-directive support and information to parents throughout the antenatal testing process. Their role is to help parents arrive at the most appropriate decision for them in the context of their family life.

ARC offers information and support to parents who:
- Are making decisions during the antenatal testing process
- Have been told that their unborn baby has an abnormality
- Are having to make difficult decisions about continuing the pregnancy
- Are having to make difficult decisions about ending the pregnancy.

185

Babyloss

Web: www.babyloss.co.uk
Email: reachout@babyloss.co.uk

The pages on this website have been collated to provide information and support online for bereaved parents whose baby has died during pregnancy, at birth or shortly afterwards.

B.A.C.P. British Association for Counselling and Psychotherapy

Tel: 0870 443 5252
Web: www.bacp.co.uk

The BACP can provide details of registered counsellors in your area, including fees.

Born too Soon

Helpline: 01977 511582 (6pm – 9pm Mon – Fri)
Web: www.borntoosoon.freeservers.com

Paula Craven, who has suffered five miscarriages, launched this site to offer support and information to anyone whose baby has died either during pregnancy or within a short time after birth.

The Child Death Helpline

Tel: 0800 282 986
Web: www.childdeathhelpline.org.uk

This helpline is run from Great Ormond Street Hospital, and is open to all.
The helpline is a listening service that offers emotional support to all those affected by the death of a child, whether family, friends or professionals. It is staffed by bereaved parents who are supervised by trained counsellors. The helpline is open 365 days a year.

Every evening 7.00 p.m. to 10.00 p.m.
Monday to Friday mornings 10.00 a.m. to 1.00 p.m.
and Wednesday afternoons 1.00 - 4.00 p.m.

The Compassionate Friends

Tel: 08451 232304
Web: www.tcf.org.uk

Compassionate Friends offer support for bereaved parents, including local groups (call number above for local contact details) and befriending. They also offer specialised support groups for grandparents, siblings and parents who have lost their only child. Their website contains many useful leaflets regarding bereavement. They also offer support where a child has taken his or her own life – Shadow of Suicide (SoS)

Cruse Bereavement Care

Tel: 0870 167 1677
Web: www.crusebereavementcare.org.uk

This national organisation offers support to anyone who is bereaved. They have local support groups (call number above for local contact details) and produce helpful resources.

The Ectopic Pregnancy Trust

Helpline: 01895 238 025
Website: www.ectopic.org.uk

The Ectopic Pregnancy Trust provides support and information to couples who have suffered an ectopic pregnancy.

FSID

Tel: 0207 2332090
Web: www.sids.org.uk/fsid

Offers support to bereaved families through its helpline, local befrienders and groups. Promotes and sponsors research into the causes and prevention of sudden and unexpected deaths (cot deaths and sudden infant death syndrome).

HeartLine Association

Tel: 01276 707636
Web: www.heartline.org.uk

Heartline is a voluntary organisation set up to offer help and support to children with heart disorders and their families regardless of how slight or severe the condition may be. They also offer support to families bereaved of a child due to a heart disorder.

The Miscarriage Association

Tel: 01924 200799 (9am to 4pm Mon – Fri)
Web: www.miscarriageassociation.org.uk

The Miscarriage Association's helpline responds to around 15,000 calls, emails and letters per year from those affected by the loss of a baby in pregnancy. They have a UK-wide network of over 150 volunteer telephone contacts who have been through pregnancy loss themselves and can offer support, understanding and a listening ear. The Miscarriage Association also has 50 support groups across the UK, where people can meet and share their experiences and feelings in a safe and supportive environment. Contact them for details of your nearest support group.

SANDS The Stillbirth and Neonatal Death Charity

Tel: 020 7436 5881
Web: www.uk-sands.org

SANDS provides support for bereaved parents and their families when their baby dies at or soon after birth. Support services include a national helpline, an internet forum, a network of over 90 local groups around the UK, and various publications.

S.O.F.T. U.K.

Tel.   0121 351 3122 for contact telephone numbers
Web: www.soft.org.uk

S.O.F.T. UK provides support, including following bereavement, for families affected by Patau's Syndrome (Trisomy 13), Edward's Syndrome (Trisomy 18) and related complications.

SOBS Survivors of Bereavement by Suicide

Tel: 0870 241 3337 (9am to 9pm every day)
Web: www.uk-sobs.org.uk

They exist to meet the needs and reduce the isolation of those bereaved by the suicide of a close relative or friend. They offer emotional and practical support in a number of ways: telephone contacts, bereavement packs, group meetings (in a number of locations), one-day conferences and residential events. They can also provide information relating to practical issues and problems. Their aim is to provide a safe, confidential environment, in which bereaved people can share their experiences and feelings, so giving and gaining support from each other.

Tamba Bereavement Support Group

Tel: 0800 138 0509
Web: www.tamba-bsg.org.uk

The Tamba BSG is a parent to parent support group and is run by bereaved parents. All BSG supporters are volunteers and are parents who have lost a child or children during a multiple pregnancy or at any stage after birth. None of the supporters are 'professionals'; they offer a befriending rather than a counselling service, although BSG does have access to professional support if required.

Resources available from the Child Bereavement Charity

Child Bereavement Charity Information Pack

Contains valuable information leaflets and suggested reading for parents and professionals alike - anyone who is involved or concerned with grieving families following the death of a baby or child and when a child is bereaved.

Grieving after the death of your baby

A book about grief following miscarriage or the death of a baby around the time of birth. It shows the many different ways parents have found to express their feelings and remember their baby. There are sections for grandparents, siblings, and if the death occurred a long time ago.

A child dies: parents' grief

A 30 minute DVD featuring four couples who talk about the death of their child and the impact on their life and their relationship.

A loss too soon

A loss too soon is a video featuring two families who share their experiences, one of the death of a baby and the other of the death of their child. It explores men's and women's reactions to loss.

A Heartbeat Away

A Heartbeat Away, compiled by Flappy Lane Fox who lost her son Harry Sidebottom, charts the journey from the isolation of grief and loss through to the first renewal of hope. This life-affirming book comprises anthologies of writings on the themes of 'Grief and Bereavement and Loss' and 'Hope, Humour and Love'.

The CBC Memory Box

To keep important items when a baby or child dies or when a child is bereaved of someone special. Clear perspex lid can be personalised and re-arranged on special occasions. Strong and durable, with compartments, to enable owners to add items over the years. Navy blue in colour, size 26.5cm x 37cm x 11cm.

My Book about our baby who died

A workbook for children 3-12 yrs, when a baby brother or sister dies at, or soon after, birth. It aims to guide parents and find ways to encourage their children to express their feelings.

When Our Baby Died - DVD

When our Baby Died has been made for parents and all who care for them. In this DVD parents explain what the death has meant to them and how it has changed their lives. They describe some of the things they have done to express their grief, mourn for their baby, and find support for themselves.
Producer Bradbury Williams SMS

Benedict A Child of Mine

A book of poems written by Alexa Warden following the death of her baby.